M000207890

"Given the explosion of the aposto[...] represents a concise and valuable survey of what is happening around the globe. Geivett and Pivec provide insightful biblical and historical analyses, which are useful for those wanting to understand these sometimes bewildering movements. Especially beneficial are the distinctions the authors make between the teachings of the historic Pentecostal churches and the more recent New Apostolic Reformation views of such leaders as C. Peter Wagner and others."

—**Vinson Synan,** Dean Emeritus,
Regent University School of Divinity

"I thank Geivett and Pivec for this book on the New Apostolic Reformation. They will be praised by some and vilified by others for writing it, but one will not, or should not, deny that they have done their work in a careful and professional manner. Here is a plea to compare claims with Scripture in a civil manner, a practice I wholeheartedly commend for all Christians regardless of their theological positions. The apostle Paul commended the Bereans for checking to see if what he was teaching complemented or contradicted the Scripture. If the apostle to the Gentiles commended this action from his hearers in the first century, one would hope that leaders of the NAR movement would see this as a biblical and prudent response to their message in the twenty-first century."

—**Karl I. Payne,** Pastor of Leadership Development and Discipleship
Training, Antioch Bible Church, Redmond, Washington;
Chaplain, Seattle Seahawks

"If you are looking for a biblically balanced, hermeneutically sound, enlightening, logical, clear, and spiritually and intellectually enriching treatment of the New Apostolic Reformation, contemporary apostles and prophets, their teachings, and the confusions surrounding these, then *God's Super-Apostles* is a must-read. It is relevant and much needed globally."

—**Sudhakar Mondithoka,** Director of Hyderabad Institute
of Theology and Apologetics (India)

"*God's Super-Apostles* is a thorough study and objective view of the New Apostolic Reformation. It is a necessary read for both traditional Pentecostals and those participating in NAR. We have needed this material for a long time."

—**Gary R. Allen,** Former Executive Editor, *Enrichment* Journal; General Council of the Assemblies of God

"Like the Bereans, who 'searched the Scriptures daily,' Geivett and Pivec encourage us to look at our church's so-called contemporary apostles and prophets and their movement called New Apostolic Reformation. Although thoroughly researched, the authors give us eye-opening details of these leaders, organizations, and their ideologies in readable English without academic jargon. The result is a very enlightening, very bold, and very cautioning volume. Every Christian must read it."

—**Varghese Thomas,** Hindustan Bible Institute and College (India)

"I am personally persuaded that, when the history of the ideas of the church at the beginning of the twentieth-first century is written in the future, Geivett's and Pivec's book *God's Super-Apostles* will become one of the most essential texts of our time. It is not only an engaging, enlivening, and critical assessment of the New Apostolic Reformation movement (without being uncharitable), but above all, timely and educational for those who want to be faithful to Scripture. A must-read for any Latin American who wants to be informed about the growth of the church of Christ in the Global South."

—**Mario Ramos-Reyes,** Director of the Institute for the Study of Culture, Ethics, and Development; Visiting Professor at the School of Law and Philosophy, Catholic University of Paraguay

"The authors clearly and systematically describe the movement's origins and outworkings, and they offer a thoughtful, balanced, and biblical counterpoint to its many errors and excesses. Their work is eminently practical, desperately needed, and long overdue."

—**Paul Carden,** Executive Director, The Center for Apologetics Research

"For centuries the church has cautiously approached identifying apostles and prophets, knowing the enormous potential for abuse that such titles offer. Geivett and Pivec capture this concern, and they rightly affirm that Pentecostals and charismatics may find themselves at particular risk of these ideas. In *God's Super-Apostles*, pastors or sincere followers of Christ can discover a valuable contribution to their need for careful discernment in their understanding of spiritual authority."

—**Mike Clarensau,** Senior Director of Healthy Church Network, General Council of the Assemblies of God

"Ever since the initial thirst for God, fostered by the Perestroika, faded, believers in the former Soviet Union have been looking for a way to expedite a new powerful awakening. Thus, many saw restoration of the apostolic and prophetic office with its promise of divine empowerment as just the missing piece of the puzzle. Unaware of the intricate history and aberrant doctrinal context of these ideas, many believers were fascinated with the stories of success. Self-proclaimed apostles—both foreign and domestic—multiplied. With their new, carefully researched, and thoroughly documented book, written in a straightforward yet tactful manner, Geivett and Pivec do a great service to the worldwide body of Christ by exposing the unorthodox nature of the New Apostolic Reformation, demonstrating its wide influence and putting its teachings and practices in the proper biblical and ethical context."

—**Dmitry Rozet,** Senior Editor, The Center for Apologetics Research

GOD'S SUPER-APOSTLES

Encountering the Worldwide Prophets and Apostles Movement

R. Douglas Geivett and Holly Pivec

WEAVER BOOK
COMPANY
WOOSTER, OHIO

God's Super-Apostles: Encountering the Worldwide Prophets and Apostles Movement
© 2014 by R. Douglas Geivett and Holly Pivec

Published by
Weaver Book Company
1190 Summerset Dr.
Wooster, OH 44691
Visit us at weaverbookcompany.com

Cover art: Mark Dobratz
Cover design: Frank Gutbrod
Editorial, design, and production:
{ In a Word } www.inawordbooks.com
/edited by Rick Matt/

Library of Congress Cataloging–in–Publication Data
Geivett, R. Douglas.
God's super-apostles: encountering the worldwide prophets and apostles movement / R. Douglas Geivett & Holly Pivec.
    pages cm.
Includes bibliographical references and index.
ISBN 978-1-941337-08-0
1. Church—Apostolicity. 2. Church polity. 3. Gifts, Spiritual. 4. Apostles.
5. Prophets. 6. Church renewal. I. Title.
BV601.2.G45 2014
270.8'3—dc23

Printed in the United States of America
14 15 16 17 18/ 5 4 3 2 1

For Kaitlyn and Erin

—Doug

For Kate and Lizzie

—Holly

Contents

Preface

by Holly

In the first century, a Jewish synagogue in the Macedonian city of Berea received a special visitor who brought new teaching. This visitor was the apostle Paul. His teaching was that Jesus—recently crucified and risen from the dead—was the Jews' long-awaited Messiah.

The people listened to Paul's new teaching with eagerness. They didn't chase him out of town and label him a false teacher for challenging their way of thinking. Rather, they showed a sincere open-mindedness about what he had to say. But they also wanted to be sure his teaching was true. These Bereans spent days searching their Scriptures to see if they supported the new teaching. After determining that they did, many became followers of Jesus.

What does this story from so long ago—found in Acts 17:10–12—have to do with the book before you? Quite a lot.

In the twenty-first century, churches in small towns and large cities throughout the world encounter teachers who, like Paul, are bringing new teaching. These teachers—part of the New Apostolic Reformation, or NAR (pronounced NAHR)—also call themselves apostles and prophets. Their teaching is that churches must submit to their leadership so they can advance God's kingdom and prepare the earth for Christ's return. Like the teaching Paul brought to Berea, the teaching of today's apostles and prophets is not unimportant. It has major effects on churches and the everyday lives of individual Christians.

So, how should Christians respond to the new NAR teaching?

The same way the Bereans did. We should hear it out with true sincerity and an open mind. We should not be quick to dismiss this teaching or to label it false just because it's new to us. We should give it a fair hearing to see if it presents important truth that we may have missed. We should also be careful to test whether the teaching is true or not. That means we should patiently search the Scriptures to see how this teaching matches up. If it does concur with the Scriptures, then we should believe it, even if it goes against our own traditions and experiences, and even if it makes us uncomfortable. But if such teaching doesn't line up with Scripture, then we must cast it aside. It's with this spirit of open-mindedness, fairness, and thoughtfulness that we've endeavored to write this book.

This is more than an academic exercise. I've wrestled passionately with specific passages of Scripture and asked God to guide me to correct understanding. In addition to studying the literature of NAR, I've attended NAR churches and conferences to hear for myself as NAR leaders delivered their teachings. And I've spent countless hours talking with people who have been part of this movement, seeking to understand it from their point of view. As a result, I sometimes found that my long-standing assumptions about certain issues were mistaken. Perhaps you will, too.

Some readers may suspect that the authors are anti-charismatic. They may expect us to argue that the miraculous gifts described in 1 Corinthians 12—including the gifts of prophesying, healing, and speaking in tongues—are no longer active in the church today. This is not our objective. Many Christians around the world, including charismatics and classical Pentecostals, believe that the miraculous gifts are still active, and we do not dispute their belief. We've tried to show that NAR teachings do not represent the views of most charismatics or classical Pentecostals, but are, rather, entirely different.

We emphasize that not all people who are affiliated with NAR hold to all the same beliefs. As with any other large, multi-faceted movement, participants in NAR hold to a spectrum of beliefs, accepting some NAR teachings and being unaware of or rejecting others. Furthermore, not all NAR leaders work together or agree on everything. When we critique a particular teaching in this book, we don't mean to imply that all NAR leaders we address hold to that same teaching. And when we use the descriptive term NAR to refer to specific leaders, books, organizations, or the like, we do not mean to imply that these leaders, books, organizations, or other entities share all the same views.

We don't address the most recent so-called manifestations of the Holy Spirit that some claim are occurring in NAR churches or the latest teachings or prophetic words supposedly spoken in these churches. The phenomena observed in some of these churches—such as the making of animal noises, Holy Laughter, and appearances of angel feathers—come and go quickly and new phenomena take their place. Even the Glory Cloud that was reportedly making appearances at Bethel Church in Redding, California, a couple of years ago has almost been forgotten now. There's a good reason that these phenomena come and go. People in NAR believe that God is always doing a new thing, and they hope not to miss out on what they refer to as the "current move of the Holy Spirit" by focusing on a "past move."

Rather than addressing each passing manifestation or latest prophetic word, we believe it will be more helpful to provide an enduring framework for understanding and evaluating NAR teachings as a whole. With this big-picture framework you'll have a better understanding of NAR than even many participants in the movement have. They may hold to a particular teaching here and another one there, but not understand how the teachings fit together into a larger theological framework that is the basis of NAR.

If you have a loved one who has been drawn into this movement and you want a brief and accurate introduction to it, or if you are simply curious and want a basic introduction for yourself, this book is for you. After reading it, if you want to know more, we encourage you to read our other book about this movement, *A New Apostolic Reformation? A Biblical Response to a Worldwide Movement* (Weaver Book Company, 2014). There we go into much greater depth in evaluating NAR teachings and describing the global influence of the movement.

We wish to express appreciation to the many individuals who helped us in various ways to research, write, and produce this book. Several did contribute to our research for sure: Todd Johnson, Vinson

Synan, Daniel Wallace, Patrick Johnstone, Gary Allen, Edmound Teo, Paul Carden, Kevin Lewis, Clint Arnold, Robert Saucy, Doug Birdsall, Gerry Breshears, Rachel Tabachnick, Alan Hultberg, Gary McIntosh, Kenneth Berding, Frank Chan, Anton Hein, and Jackie Alnor. Others read the manuscript and made many helpful suggestions: Craig Dorsheimer, Sherina Anderson, Rebecca Worthen, Jacquelyne Clevenger, and Kaitlyn Geivett. Ron Rhodes and Norman Geisler encouraged us to press on. Of course, their assistance in no way implies that they fully agree with all our conclusions.

We also thank all those who generously shared their personal stories with us about their experiences in NAR. We've changed their names to protect their privacy, but they know who they are, and we want them to know of our gratitude.

We're also grateful to Jim Weaver at Weaver Book Company for asking us to write this introduction to NAR. His grace and professionalism have been an inspiration to us. Emily Varner brought her marketing expertise and enthusiasm to our project and was a joy to work with, as was Alexander Bukovietski and his production team, including our copyeditor, Rick Matt. We owe a special debt of gratitude to Mark Dobratz, the cover artist, and to Frank Gutbrod, the cover designer. A special thanks to John Muether and David Veldkamp for creating the indexes.

Doug thanks John's Place, "our friendly neighborhood diner, where I was always welcome to park and work on our book."

Holly would like to thank Doug for seeing the importance of this project and partnering with her in it. He has been more than a co-author, but also a mentor, and Holly feels privileged to work with him. She also thanks her church family, Bethel Church in Fairbanks, Alaska, including the pastors and their wives, the members of her small group, and Cheryl Sackett. Holly is grateful to her supportive family, including her late father, Herb, who was one of her biggest encouragers. She especially thanks her husband, Adam, for his patience, encouragement, and insightful critique of her thinking and writing.

1

What Is the New Apostolic Reformation?

Although Mark was raised in a Christian home, he always felt like his Christian life was lacking something—something more fulfilling and exciting than the usual Bible study and Christian service. As he was finishing college, he met some people who urged him to attend a church led by an influential apostle. He did, and found what he'd been looking for in the form of dreams, divine revelations, and supernatural experiences.

You might think Mark's newfound passion for his faith would please his parents. But his loyalty to the apostle and his church has severely strained his relationship with his father, Steve. Steve feels hurt because Mark seems to think he's spiritually superior to his parents who haven't adopted his "fuller" version of Christianity. There's a spiritual distance between father and son that wasn't there before.

To make matters more painful, Steve learned that his daughter-in-law, Jan, was told by prophets associated with their church that an evil generational curse had been passed on to her husband, Mark, through Steve's family line. Steve fears that Mark and Jan may try to keep their two children away from their grandparents because of their concern that a curse is on Steve. Only by following the divine guidance of their new church leaders will Mark and Jan be able to undo the curse, they believe. In this case, the cost may include a severed relationship with Mark's parents.

★★★

Robert, a Christian for thirty-two years, was an elder at a Pentecostal church. He grew concerned about some prophets that began influencing the church with teachings he believed were clearly unbiblical.

Through his own teaching opportunities at church, he began challenging the prophets' claims. But his pastor told him to stop, explaining that his first priority as a pastor was to keep everyone in his
church at peace. Robert eventually felt he had no choice but to leave
the church he loved and where he had served for twenty-five years.
The move was emotionally painful for him. "I felt like I was getting
a divorce," he says.

★★★

Jake used to follow contemporary apostles and prophets, but now he
believes their teachings to be false. Jake says he feels free, knowing he
no longer needs to seek greater spiritual enlightenment or supernatural powers—or to convince other Christians that that's what they
need to do as well. But he still struggles with doubt. That's because
one of the well-known prophets he used to follow predicted that,
in the end time, a Great Christian Civil War will be fought in the
church between God's true followers and those who oppose them.[1]
This way of thinking was deep-seated for Jake. He fears that he may
find himself fighting on the wrong side during this war. His friends
haven't helped matters any. They call him a Pharisee for challenging
the teachings of the apostles and prophets. Jake says, "It's been very
hard, heartbreaking, and confusing as God has been bringing me out
of this way of thinking."

★★★

These three stories, all of them true, share a common thread. The path
of a new religious movement led by apostles and prophets is strewn
with confused people, divided churches, and strained families as people are forced to make painful choices between those they love and
what they believe to be the truth of God's Word. This movement is
known as the New Apostolic Reformation (NAR, pronounced NAHR).

---

[1]   The prophet Rick Joyner wrote about this Great Christian Civil War
in his bestselling book *The Final Quest* (Charlotte, NC: MorningStar Publications, 1996), 22.

If you thought apostles and prophets only lived way back in Bible times and have long since disappeared, think again. Contemporary people calling themselves apostles and prophets have many followers. They are vigorously active in churches in the United States and throughout the world. Odds are, some are active in your own community. These men and women claim they have the God-given authority, divine strategies, and miraculous powers needed to advance God's earthly kingdom so that Christ can return. And they offer people a choice.

If you submit to their leadership, then you too will work mighty miracles. You'll become part of a great end-time army that will bring about a world revival and cleanse the earth of evil by calling down hailstones, fire, and the other judgments of God described in the New Testament book of Revelation.

If you do not submit to their leadership then, at the very least, you will miss out on God's end-time plans. And if you actively oppose the apostles and prophets, then brace yourself for the fallout. Others must be warned that you are the pawn of a powerful demon, known as the "spirit of religion."[2]

This may sound radical and unappealing, but NAR is growing rapidly. In the United States, it began taking off in the 1980s and 1990s, when prophets and apostles starting showing up in churches. Today, about three million people in the United States attend churches that openly embrace NAR apostles and prophets.[3] And that number doesn't include the many Pentecostal and charismatic churches that have not openly embraced these leaders, yet have been influenced

---

[2] C. Peter Wagner claims that people who object to NAR are under the influence of a powerful demon known as the "corporate spirit of religion" or also as the "spirit of religion." See C. Peter Wagner, *Changing Church* (Ventura, CA: Regal Books, 2004), 18–21. See Appendix C of our book for other ways objectors are demonized by NAR leaders.

[3] Todd Johnson of the Center for the Study of Global Christianity at Gordon-Conwell Theological Seminary provided this estimate in a personal communication with one of the authors.

by their teachings in varying degrees. People in these churches read bestselling books by NAR prophets—books like Rick Joyner's *The Final Quest* or the apostle Bill Johnson's *When Heaven Invades Earth*. Or they use a new, wildly popular NAR Bible, called *The Passion Translation*, produced by the apostle Brian Simmons, who claims that Christ visited him personally and commissioned him to release this new translation.[4]

And we haven't yet mentioned NAR churches in other parts of the world where the movement is growing most swiftly—Africa, Asia, and Latin America.

In short, NAR is a global movement with an agenda to bring back apostles and prophets to the church—apostles like Peter and Paul and prophets like Moses and Elijah. NAR leaders claim that God always intended for apostles and prophets to govern the church, not only the early church, but the church during each generation. Yet their rightful place of rule has been neglected by Christians for centuries. Instead of apostles and prophets, today's churches are usually governed by pastors and elders.

NAR leaders call their new movement *apostolic* because they claim to be restoring apostles and prophets to the church. And they call it a *reformation* because they say it will completely change the way church is done—and its effects will be greater than the sixteenth-century Protestant Reformation.

That's a bold claim. Yet many people who are part of this movement don't know it's called the New Apostolic Reformation. In fact, they may not even know they are part of a movement at all. And they may not be fully aware of all the extreme teachings associated with it. But they certainly know of—and follow the teachings of—men and women who believe they are apostles and prophets similar to the apostles of Christ and the Old Testament prophets.

---

[4]   See Brian Simmons, "Song of Solomon, Part 1," *Passion for Jesus Conference*, YouTube video, 51:29, posted by HealingWaters, February 19, 2012; accessed June 18, 2014, https://www.youtube.com/watch?v=H8pmNZnl-zIA.

INFLUENTIAL APOSTLES, PROPHETS, AND NAR TEACHERS

NAR is not a single organization, but a movement of independent churches, organizations, and leaders. Since it's not a formal organization, there are no official lists of NAR churches or leaders. Nor is there an official list of beliefs. What ties those associated with the movement together is their belief in contemporary apostles and prophets.

Most NAR apostles, prophets, and teachers are not known outside their own networks of churches or the local regions where they operate. However, a number of influential individuals energetically promote today's prophets and apostles, and many even claim to be apostles or prophets themselves. Some who are well known include:

- C. Peter Wagner and Chuck Pierce (Global Spheres in Corinth, Texas)
- Rick Joyner (MorningStar Ministries in Fort Mill, South Carolina)
- Bill Johnson and Kris Vallotton (Bethel Church in Redding, California)
- Cindy Jacobs (Generals International in Red Oak, Texas)
- Mike Bickle (International House of Prayer in Kansas City, Missouri)
- Dutch Sheets (Dutch Sheets Ministries in Dallas, Texas)
- Ché Ahn (HRock Church in Pasadena, California)
- James W. Goll (prophet for Harvest International Ministry and author of the bestselling book *The Seer*)
- Mark Chironna (Church on the Living Edge in Longwood, Florida)
- Bill Hamon (Christian International Ministries Network in Santa Rosa Beach, Florida)
- Lou Engle (The Call prayer and fasting rallies)
- Kim Clement (Kim Clement Center in Tulsa, Oklahoma)
- Randy Clark (Global Awakening in Mechanicsburg, Pennsylvania)

WELL-KNOWN NAR ORGANIZATIONS AND MEDIA OUTLETS

Some US organizations led by NAR leaders include:

- The International House of Prayer (IHOP) in Kansas City, Missouri
- Bethel Church in Redding, California
- The Call (stadium-sized prayer and fasting rallies)
- Aglow International in Edmonds, Washington
- Healing Rooms Ministries in Spokane, Washington
- MorningStar Ministries in Fort Mill, South Carolina
- Christian International Ministries Network in Santa Rosa Beach, Florida
- GOD TV
- Trinity Broadcasting Network
- *Charisma* magazine
- The Elijah List (http://www.elijahlist.com)
- Identity Network (http://www.identitynetwork.net)

2

NAR Apostles: The Generals

An influential apostle stood on stage before members of the large church he pastors in Southern California. The apostle told of a man who came to him offering a large sum of money. Surprised by the gesture, he told the man, "That's a lot of money." The man replied, "I want to give it to you. You're my apostle." The apostle then agreed that it was appropriate to accept the money. He recalled the story in Acts 4:34–37, about members of the early church who brought all their money and laid it at the feet of Christ's apostles.

Although this apostle was initially surprised by the man's action, his acceptance of this generous gift sent a message to others. They, too, should give of their resources to this apostle since he is their local spiritual authority.

As the apostle recounted the story, a young man in the audience suddenly stood up. With confusion written on his face, he said, tentatively, but loud enough for all to hear, "Something is not right here. Something is just not right."

The young man's voice wasn't angry. He simply seemed baffled, like he was trying to sort out what was wrong about what was going on. The apostle looked at him and said, "You're out of order." A couple of burly men quickly escorted the young man out of the building. The apostle continued on, as if the interruption never happened.

While some in the audience may have forgotten about the incident, at least one person, Liam, still remembers. Most of the people saw a young man who, by questioning the authority of a respected apostle, acted rebelliously. But Liam saw someone who didn't seem rebellious at all, but rather genuinely alarmed.

Why was he alarmed? Though he couldn't quite put his finger on it, the young man seemed to sense something unbiblical about the way the apostle exerted authority over the people in the church.

This scene plays out in NAR churches throughout the world. And it goes to the heart of NAR teachings. It raises the question: Are there apostles today who share a level of authority similar to Christ's original apostles?

Many people active in NAR say yes. Most other Christians say no.

In this chapter we explain NAR teachings about apostles. In the next chapter, we review what the Bible teaches about apostles. And in chapter 4 we evaluate NAR teachings in light of the Bible's teachings.

THE MAIN NAR TEACHING ON APOSTLES: THEY MUST GOVERN

The main NAR teaching about apostles, which sets the movement apart from the views of other Christians, is that they must govern the church. By govern, we mean that they direct the church in an authoritative way.

NAR apostles claim they hold a formal office in church government like the office of pastor or elder. Except the apostle's office wields much more authority than these other offices because an apostle has jurisdiction over multiple churches, and not mere oversight of a single church. And an apostle's authority can extend beyond churches to cities and workplaces, and among institutions that have no connection with the church.

Many NAR leaders teach that apostles hold the most important office in the church. They are the equivalent of generals. All other church leaders in what they call their apostolic network—including pastors—are expected to submit to the apostles' authority.

In contrast to this novel and revolutionary NAR view of apostles, Protestant Christians typically don't believe that contemporary apostles must govern churches. They believe instead that the governing office of apostle was a temporary office in the early church held by a special class of apostles—those appointed directly by the resurrected Lord and including the Twelve and Paul. The apostles' main tasks included establishing the first churches and overseeing the writing of New Testament Scripture. After completing these tasks, the need for the office of apostle—with its extraordinary authority to govern—was fulfilled.

Sometimes Protestants have referred to pioneering missionaries as apostles—those who were the first to take the gospel to unreached lands, such as William Carey (India) and Hudson Taylor (China). And many Pentecostals and charismatics[1] refer to contemporary missionaries and church planters as apostles, and even believe that these apostles will perform miraculous signs to confirm the truth of the gospel they proclaim. But, like other Protestants, Pentecostals and charismatics typically do not believe these missionary, miracle-working apostles must govern the church.[2]

The authority claimed by many NAR apostles is far greater than the authority claimed by most church leaders outside the movement. Outside NAR, authority to direct churches is generally vested in *groups* of worthy leaders rather than in individuals; these may be groups of elders or the groups of voting members in a congregation.

----

[1] We use the term *Pentecostals* to refer to people who are members of a classical Pentecostal denomination such as the Assemblies of God. We use the term *charismatics* to refer to people who are not members of a classical Pentecostal denomination but do emphasize the miraculous gifts of the Holy Spirit, such as speaking in tongues, prophesying, and the working of miracles. These people can be found within mainline, non-Pentecostal denominations or in independent charismatic churches.

[2] The Assemblies of God, the world's largest Pentecostal denomination, has issued official statements against NAR teachings. See "Apostles and Prophets," General Presbytery of the Assemblies of God, August 6, 2001; accessed June 19, 2014, http://ag.org/top/Beliefs/Position_Papers/pp_downloads/pp_4195_apostles_prophets.pdf; also "End-Time Revival—Spirit-Led and Spirit-Controlled: A Response Paper to Resolution 16," General Presbytery of the Assemblies of God, August 11, 2000; accessed June 19, 2014, http://ag.org/top/Beliefs/Position_Papers/pp_downloads/pp_end-time_revival.pdf.

The authority claimed by NAR apostles is greater even than the authority of Roman Catholic bishops, who exercise their governing authority in submission to the ultimate authority of the pope.

NAR leaders are bold in granting extraordinary authority to their apostles. Apostle C. Peter Wagner, one of the most influential apostles in the United States, declares, "Of all the changes involved with the emergence of the New Apostolic Reformation, the most radical of all is the following: *the recognition of the amount of spiritual authority delegated by the Holy Spirit to individuals"* (Wagner's emphasis).[3]

How does that individual authority play out? In a NAR church on the local level, the senior pastor is viewed as the leader of the church. But in an apostolic network—where the pastors of multiple churches have submitted to the authority of a single apostle—the apostle oversees the pastors collectively and casts the vision for the entire network. When apostles determine it to be necessary, they may intervene directly in the affairs of the local churches, disciplining members, settling disputes, and correcting pastors' doctrine.

A pastor—who is a church's local authority—submits to the authority of an apostle when the pastor voluntarily joins an apostolic network. A pastor also agrees that his or her church will contribute financially to the apostolic network. For example, Harvest International Ministry (HIM), an apostolic network of more than 20,000 churches under the direction of US apostle Ché Ahn, expects churches in its network to make a monthly donation; the recommended donation is between five and ten percent of the church's monthly gross income.[4]

Pastors of individual churches must submit to apostles because pastors aren't authorized to advance God's kingdom on a grand scale. As Wagner puts it, "The responsibility of pastors is to care for, nurture and comfort the flock. Very few pastors have either the gifts or the

---

[3] C. Peter Wagner, *The Church in the Workplace: How God's People Can Transform Society* (Ventura, CA: Regal Books, 2006), 25.

[4] "Ministry Assumptions," Harvest International Ministry, accessed March 18, 2014, http://harvestim.org/index.php?a=about&s=membership&ss=ministry-assumptions.

temperament to mobilize an army for war. Apostles, on the other hand, do."[5]

The NAR practice of submitting to an apostle is referred to as seeking spiritual covering (or spiritual protection) under the authority of an apostle.[6] This practice is also referred to as seeking apostolic covering. All pastors, other church leaders, and individuals are expected to seek the spiritual covering of an apostle. Pastors submit to apostles by joining apostolic networks. And individuals submit to apostles by joining a church that is part of an apostolic network.

But why would *pastors* seek spiritual covering? One reason is that they need apostles to make it possible for them to obey God's call on their lives. Or, as Wagner says, "They are convinced that they would not be able to reach their full destiny in serving God apart from the spiritual covering of the apostle."[7]

And why would *individuals* seek spiritual covering? They're taught that God promises protection and blessing to those who submit to all God-given authority, including the authority of apostles. This teaching is promoted by many NAR leaders, including bestselling author John Bevere in his book *Under Cover: The Promise of Protection Under His Authority.*[8]

There is an especially urgent reason people in NAR seek spiritual covering. Their willingness to submit to an apostle is seen as a litmus test of their submission to God. Failure to submit to an apostle is seen as defiance against God. As prophet-apostle Bill Hamon warns, "It is almost impossible for individuals to humble themselves under

---

[5]   C. Peter Wagner, *Dominion! How Kingdom Action Can Change the World* (Grand Rapids: Chosen Books, 2008), 123.

[6]   See the definition of *covering* in Abraham S. Rajah, *Apostolic and Prophetic Dictionary: Language of the End-Time Church* (Bloomington, IN: WestBow Press, 2013), 20.

[7]   C. Peter Wagner, *Changing Church* (Ventura, CA: Regal Books, 2004), 36.

[8]   John Bevere, *Under Cover: The Promise of Protection Under His Authority* (Nashville: Thomas Nelson, 2001).

God without humbling themselves in submission and relationship to Christ's delegated representatives of Him to His Church."[9]

Pay close attention to Hamon's words. They explain why many people in NAR are afraid to challenge the words of an apostle or to attend a church that is not under the authority of an apostle.

Anyone who does not submit to the authority of an apostle is at risk. This is because an apostle's authority comes directly from God. So the failure to recognize a true apostle is a serious matter. Wagner writes: "On that point let me make a strong statement: *To the degree that the Corinthian believers did not recognize that the Lord had made Paul an apostle, they were out of the will of God!* That would have been a dangerous place to be!"[10] The same goes for failure to recognize the apostles today.

KEY BIBLE PASSAGES USED TO DEFEND NAR TEACHING ON APOSTLES

The three major proof-texts used to defend NAR teaching that apostles must govern the church are Ephesians 4:11–13, Ephesians 2:20, and 1 Corinthians 12:28.

Ephesians 4:11–13

The passage of Scripture most often cited to support NAR teaching about apostolic government of the church today is Ephesians 4:11–13:

> And he gave the apostles, the prophets, the evangelists, the shepherds and teachers, to equip the saints for the work of ministry, for building up the body of Christ, until we all attain to the unity of the faith and of the

[9] Bill Hamon, *Apostles, Prophets, and the Coming Moves of God: God's End-Time Plans for His Church and Planet Earth* (Santa Rosa Beach, FL: Destiny Image Publishers, 1997), 153.

[10] Wagner's emphasis. C. Peter Wagner, *Apostles Today: Biblical Government for Biblical Power* (Ventura, CA: Regal Books, 2006), 25.

knowledge of the Son of God, to mature manhood, to the measure of the stature of the fullness of Christ.

In the NAR understanding of this passage, Jesus, at his ascension to heaven, gave the church five governing offices: apostle, prophet, evangelist, pastor (shepherd), and teacher. Verse 13, they say, clearly indicates that these five governing offices are not temporal, but ongoing because they must build up—or equip—the church *until* it reaches spiritual maturity. Wagner writes, "Who in their right mind can claim that we have arrived at that point? The only reasonable conclusion is that we are still in need of all five offices."[11]

This NAR teaching is often referred to as the fivefold ministry teaching. Churches that do not have apostles or prophets, but only evangelists, pastors, and teachers, are like a hand that is missing two fingers. Only when a church has all five offices will it become God's powerful hand to advance his kingdom.

Ephesians 2:20

A second NAR favorite is Ephesians 2:20:

[The church is] built on the foundation of the apostles and prophets, Christ Jesus himself being the cornerstone.

Wagner believes that Ephesians 4:11 teaches that apostles have ongoing, equipping roles in the church. And he believes that Ephesians 2:20 makes it clear that these apostles hold governmental offices. As he says, "Equipping the saints is one thing, but some will say that is not necessarily governing. True, so let's go back a couple of chapters to Ephesians 2:20, where Paul describes the church as the 'household of God.' . . . According to this Scripture, after He ascended and sent the Holy Spirit, He left the nuts and bolts of building the church to the leadership of apostles and prophets."[12]

---

[11]   Ibid., 13.

[12]   Wagner, *The Church in the Workplace*, 23.

1 Corinthians 12:28

A third passage used to defend the teaching that apostles must govern the church is 1 Corinthians 12:28:

> *And God has appointed in the church first apostles, second prophets, third teachers, then miracles, then gifts of healing, helping, administrating, and various kinds of tongues.*

According to Wagner, this verse teaches that apostles today occupy the "first" office in the "order or sequence" of church government.[13] But since contemporary apostles have not, historically, been recognized in Protestant churches, teachers (pastors) have wrongly risen to the first position in church government. Wagner says, "It is fascinating that even though we have had church government backward over the past two centuries according to 1 Corinthians 12:28, we have evangelized so much of the world! Think of what will happen now that church government is getting in proper order."[14]

It might seem that NAR leaders have made a biblical case that contemporary apostles must govern the church. We'll evaluate their interpretations of these Scriptures in chapter 4 and show where they go wrong. But first we describe the responsibilities of NAR apostles.

What NAR Apostles Do

Many different types of apostles can be found in NAR, including especially important ecclesiastical apostles who govern churches and ministries, and critically strategic workplace apostles who govern the church in the workplace—that is, they govern the Christians who work in various sectors of society, like business, media, and government.

How does someone become an apostle in NAR? First, such a person will exhibit will several publicly recognizable characteristics of an

---

[13]   Wagner, *Apostles Today*, 12.

[14]   Ibid.

apostle so that others will acknowledge a claim to apostolic authority. That person will then be publicly commissioned—or affirmed—as an apostle by other apostles during an official ceremony.

What are the characteristics of an apostle? Apostles are authorized by God to do many things.[15] An apostle will:

- receive revelation directly from God and from prophets;
- cast new vision for the church based on the revelation the apostle has received;
- birth (or start) new ministries;
- lead the church in spiritual warfare;
- teach;
- impart or activate spiritual gifts in individuals;
- initiate and carry out projects to advance God's kingdom by strategizing and fundraising;
- complete projects by bringing them to desired conclusions to advance God's kingdom;
- send out others who are equipped to fulfill their roles in expanding the kingdom of God; and
- raise up future leadership.

Other things are true for many, but not all, contemporary apostles.[16] They will:

- have seen Jesus personally;
- perform supernatural manifestations, such as miraculous signs and wonders;
- expose heresy;
- plant new churches within their apostolic network;

---

[15] This list is adapted from lists in Wagner, *Apostles Today*, 28–34, 146–47.

[16] Ibid., 30–33, 147. Wagner's book includes two lists of the things many apostles do. They contain some differences. Our list merges both of Wagner's. Notice that Wagner does not give clear explanations of what he means by many items in the list, such as "break curses of witchcraft." Also notice that Wagner writes that some NAR leaders will disagree with his assessment of certain apostolic functions as being optional.

- appoint and oversee local church pastors;
- settle disputes in the church;
- impose church discipline, including excommunication;
- provide spiritual covering for other leaders;
- suffer physical persecution;
- attract and distribute financial resources within the network of churches they govern;
- minister cross-culturally;
- fast frequently;
- take back territory from the enemy and transfer it to the kingdom of God;
- cast out demons; and
- break curses of witchcraft.

Apostles do other things as well, but these are seen as their most important functions for advancing God's kingdom.

★★★

In summary, NAR apostles are viewed as the generals in the church. NAR leaders teach that all churches and individual Christians must submit to their leadership if they wish to experience God's protection and blessing. Those who do not submit are seen as rebels against God.

INTERNATIONAL COALITION OF APOSTOLIC LEADERS (ICAL)

This coalition—formerly named the International Coalition of Apostles—is the largest network of apostles in the world, made up of approximately four hundred apostles from forty-five nations. Founded in 1999, it is presently led by convening apostle John P. Kelly of Colleyville, Texas, and was previously led by Peter Wagner. Membership is restricted to those who receive a formal invitation from the convening apostle after being nominated by two members. The annual membership fee for a US apostle, as of December 2013, was $450.

This coalition stopped making its membership list available to the public in 2010.[a] In years prior to that time, some influential people who were named as apostles in the coalition included:[b]

- Jane Hansen Hoyt of Aglow International
- Cal Pierce of Healing Rooms Ministries
- Chris Hayward of Cleansing Streams Ministries
- E. H. Jim Ammerman of Chaplaincy Full Gospel Churches
- David Shibley of Global Advance
- Samuel Rodriguez of National Hispanic Christian Leadership Conference
- Héctor Torres of Hispanic International Ministries
- J. Doug Stringer of Somebody Cares International
- Stephen Strang of Charisma Media
- J. Lee Grady of Charisma magazine
- Dick Eastman of Every Home for Christ
- Harold Caballeros, former minister of foreign affairs of Guatemala
- Ed Silvoso of Harvest Evangelism
- Ted Haggard, former president of the National Association of Evangelicals

In association with ICAL, other coalitions of apostles have formed around the world, including the European Coalition of Apostolic Leaders (led by convener Jan-Aage Torp), and 45 national coalitions, including:

- the Nigerian Coalition of Apostles
- the Brazilian Coalition of Apostles
- the Canadian Coalition of Apostles
- the Indonesian Coalition of Apostles
- the Australian Coalition of Apostles and Prophets

a.   The website Talk to Action has compiled a collection of membership lists from previous years. See "International Coalition of Apostles Membership Lists," Talk to Action, September 3, 2011; accessed December 19, 2013, http://www.talk-2action.org/story/2011/9/3/9571/00192.

b.   We note that past involvement by individuals with this council , or any other NAR group, need not indicate that they are NAR themselves. They may not have known at the time of their initial involvement what the council's purposes and objectives are; the council also may have evolved and become more easily identifiable as NAR later on.

3

Apostles in the Bible: A Close Look

Now that we've looked at NAR teachings on apostles, let's review what the Bible teaches about them.

THE TWELVE APOSTLES

The first group of apostles to appear in the Bible was the twelve apostles. At the beginning of Jesus' earthly ministry, he chose twelve men to be his special inner circle of disciples to learn from him and to minister with him. These men were Simon Peter, Andrew, James, John, Philip, Bartholomew, Thomas, Matthew, James, Thaddeus, Simon the Zealot, and Judas Iscariot (Matt. 10:2–4).

The first time Jesus referred to his twelve disciples as *apostles*—which, in the Greek, means "ones who are sent"—was when he sent them to preach the "kingdom of heaven" to the Israelites (Matt. 10:2). Eventually they became known collectively as the Twelve. Following his resurrection, Jesus sent the Twelve—minus Judas, who betrayed Jesus and killed himself and was replaced by Matthias—to preach the gospel to all nations (Matt. 28:16–20). Thus, the twelve disciples became apostles when they were sent by Christ to fulfill a special mission.

The Unique Role of the Twelve

While it's true that all followers of Christ from the beginning until now are his disciples and have also been sent to preach the gospel to all nations, the twelve apostles played a unique role in founding the early church. They served as official eyewitnesses of Jesus' entire earthly ministry, and were the first to see Jesus alive after his resurrection.

Not just anybody could qualify for membership in this group. For example, following the resurrection, the eleven remaining disciples determined that they should find a substitute for Judas. This would complete the circle of twelve. The apostle Peter specified that the man they selected must be someone like themselves, *who had been an eyewitness of Jesus' entire earthly ministry* (Acts 1:21–22), all the way from his baptism to his ascension into heaven.

The unique role of these eyewitnesses can also be seen in a sermon Peter later preached to a group of Gentiles:

> *We are witnesses of all that he [Jesus] did both in the country of the Jews and in Jerusalem. They put him to death by hanging him on a tree, but God raised him on the third day and made him to appear, not to all the people but to us who had been chosen by God as witnesses, who ate and drank with him after he rose from the dead.* (Acts 10:39–41)

The Functions of the Twelve

As the official eyewitnesses of Jesus' earthly ministry, the twelve apostles had three main functions.

They Were to Proclaim the Resurrection

As the uniquely appointed eyewitnesses of Jesus' earthly ministry, the Twelve proclaimed the resurrection (Acts 2). They also performed miraculous signs and wonders that confirmed their status as God's special messengers (Acts 2:43; 3:4–8; 5:12; 6:1–6).

They Were to Govern the Church

As an institution, the Twelve—who were headquartered in Jerusalem—were the earliest leaders in the church (Acts 1:15–26; 2:14–47; 4:32–37). When the church grew too large for this band of apostles to govern the details, they appointed deacons to oversee administrative tasks (Acts 5:1–11). But the twelve apostles continued to have special, superior authority in the early church—not only at Jerusalem, but also among churches planted in other regions. Thus this period came to be called the Apostolic Age. The authority of the Twelve is seen in their dispatch of a delegation of two of their members—Peter and John—to Samaria. Their aim was to verify that the Samaritans had indeed received the gospel and had become part of God's people. The authority of the Twelve is seen also in the way churches looked to them to resolve doctrinal disputes, such as the notorious controversy taken up at the Council at Jerusalem (Acts 15:2, 6, 22–23).

They Were to Write Scripture

Their companionship with Jesus from the beginning and their eye-witness testimony concerning all that he had said and taught were rightly judged to make the apostles uniquely authoritative. This authority extended to their writing under the inspiration of the Holy Spirit. The New Testament had the same authority as the undisputed authority of the Hebrew Scriptures (the Old Testament). Their teachings and writings were continually sought by the first believers (Acts 2:42).

Before his crucifixion, Jesus alluded to the apostles' future role in writing Scripture. He spoke of the Helper—that is, the Holy Spirit—whom he would send to help them testify about Jesus and remember all the things he had taught them (John 14:26; 15:26–27). Their divinely inspired accounts of Jesus' ministry became the four New Testament Gospels—Matthew, Mark, Luke, and John.

The apostles Matthew and John wrote the Gospels bearing their names. John Mark, the probable author of Mark, was not an apostle, but it is generally believed that he received the material for his Gospel from the apostle Peter. In this way his report had the authority of an apostle. Nor was Luke an apostle. In the introduction to his Gospel, however, he explicitly says that he received his material from "those who from the beginning were eyewitnesses" (Luke 1:2)—those eye-witnesses would naturally have included the twelve apostles, Christ's official eyewitnesses. Both Mark and Luke, then, recognized that their accounts must be properly authorized by the apostles.

Besides the Gospels, other books of Scripture were written by the apostles Peter and John: the first and second letters of Peter to the church at large, three letters by John (also distributed to the churches), and the book of Revelation (written by John at the end of his life).

While Matthew, John, and Peter are the only members of the Twelve who actually penned documents of Scripture, the entire group functioned to preserve, transmit, and certify the authentic teachings of Jesus. When books were being recognized as Scripture in the early centuries of the church, those that were written by one or another of the Twelve—or by their close associates, like Mark and Luke—were safely judged to be divinely inspired. As such, they bore the stamp of approval from Jesus' authorized eyewitnesses, those he specially commissioned as apostles. And, by extension, these books had the authority of Jesus himself.

The Apostle Paul

Besides the twelve apostles, the most influential apostle in the early church was Paul.

The Twelve were sent as apostles when Jesus appeared to them in the forty days following his resurrection (Acts 1:3–8). This was before Jesus ascended into heaven. But Paul was not yet a follower of Christ at that time, and could not have been sent as an apostle until sometime later—at least one or two years after the ascension and perhaps as many as several years later. In due course, Jesus Christ, the ascended Lord, confronted Paul and commissioned him to preach the gospel to the Gentiles (Acts 26:16–18).

Paul's Apostolic Uniqueness

Paul's encounter with the risen Christ resulted in his immediate and radical conversion. The once violent persecutor of Jesus' followers would become one of their most influential leaders. He came to see himself above all as an "apostle to the Gentiles" (Rom. 11:13, see also Rom. 1:5; Gal. 1:16; 2:7–9). He believed that God had called him to this unique role even before he was born, just as God had called the Old Testament prophets Isaiah and Jeremiah to their own unique roles before they were born (Gal. 1:15–16).

Paul was keenly aware that his commission occurred at an abnormally late point in time as compared with the other apostles. In recounting the many appearances Christ made after his resurrection, in the order of their occurrence, he wrote:

> [H]e appeared to Cephas [Peter], then to the twelve. Then he appeared to more than five hundred brothers at one time, most of whom are still alive, though some have fallen asleep. Then he appeared to James, then to all the apostles. Last of all, as to one untimely born, he appeared also to me. For I am the least of the apostles, unworthy to be called an apostle, because I persecuted the church of God. (1 Cor. 15:5–9)

By referring to himself as "one untimely born," Paul acknowledged that the timing of Christ's appearance to him was, in comparison with other apostles, a departure from the norm. It didn't occur in the days immediately following Christ's resurrection—at the time when Jesus appeared to the Twelve and "all the apostles." The unusually late timing indicated that Paul was a unique apostle and that he had a particular role to fulfill.

Paul also stated in verse 8 of the same passage that Christ appeared to him "last of all." This indicates that Paul was the last person to whom Christ made a first-time appearance.[1] Since seeing the resurrected Christ is a requirement for apostleship (1 Cor. 9:1), Paul's remark in 1 Corinthians 15:9 suggests that he saw himself as being the last and final apostle—at least the last of a certain type of apostle. And during this last appearance, Jesus clearly commissioned Paul to exercise special authority in the founding of his church. This commission would later be confirmed through Paul's association with the other apostles of Christ.

---

[1] Jesus later appeared to John (Rev. 1:9–17), but John had already been with Jesus, both before and after the resurrection.

Paul's Apostolic Functions

Announcing the Next Stage in Salvation History

As an apostle to the Gentiles, Paul was authorized to announce the next stage in salvation history, the time when the gospel began to be preached not only to the Jews, but also equally to the Gentiles (Rom. 1:16). In addition to his authorization to announce this development in salvation history, he was to play a strategic role in launching and carrying it out. In preaching the gospel to the Gentiles, Paul led extensive missionary campaigns directed toward Gentiles. He traveled across the ancient world, preaching the gospel and planting churches. His message was confirmed by God with miraculous signs and wonders (Acts 14:3; 19:11–12; Rom. 15:19). And his ministry bore much fruit.

Governing the Church

Like the Twelve, Paul also exercised great authority over churches. This is seen in his freedom to issue commands and stern warnings to the churches, sometimes including threats of discipline (see, for example, 1 Cor. 5:4–5; 2 Cor. 13:2, 10). Paul even asserted apostolic authority over churches he hadn't founded, as can be seen in his letter to the Romans. And the Twelve acknowledged Paul's authority over the churches, which is evident in the way that Peter referred to Paul's letters as "Scriptures" (2 Peter 3:16).

Writing Scripture

Paul's most important function was writing Scripture. He received a number of revelations directly from Christ, including insight into the mystery of Jews and Gentiles being united in the church (Eph. 3:3–6). This revelation, along with Paul's instructions for the early Christians and his other teachings, was contained in letters he sent to churches under his oversight. These letters were ultimately compiled with other apostolic documents to form the New Testament. In fact, Paul

wrote more books of the New Testament than any other author—
thirteen of the twenty-seven canonical books.[2]

THE OTHER APOSTLES

The Twelve and Paul are the most influential apostles in the New
Testament. But others are also referred to as apostles. Very little information is provided about them, however.

One mentioned by name is Barnabas (Acts 13:2–3; 14:4, 14;
1 Cor. 9:6). Others who may have been called apostles—depending on how certain verses are rendered—include James the half-
brother of Jesus (1 Cor. 15:7; Gal. 1:19; 2:9), Andronicus and Junia
(Rom. 16:7), other unnamed half-brothers of Christ (1 Cor. 9:5), and
Silas (Acts 15:40; 1 Thess. 2:6).[3]

At least some of these individuals had important roles in the early
church. Barnabas was a recognized leader in the church at Antioch
and an effective missionary and church planter. Andronicus and Junia are described, by no less an authority than Paul, as "outstanding
among the apostles" (Rom. 16:7, NIV). James was an influential leader in the Jerusalem Church and the author of a book of Scripture
that is named after him (the epistle of James). The judgment he issued

---

[2] Some Bible scholars believe that Paul also wrote Hebrews, though
the majority of scholars today doubt this. If he did write Hebrews, that
would bring the total number of Pauline letters to fourteen.

[3] Bible translators have differed in their renderings of verses that mention these individuals; some translators believe these verses refer to the individuals as apostles, and others do not. For example, Andronicus and Junias,
in Romans 16:17, are said to be "outstanding among the apostles" in the
translation of this verse provided in the New International Version. But they
are said to be "well known to the apostles" in the translation given in the
English Standard Version. Some scholars who argue that it was doubtful
that Andronicus and Junia were apostles are Michael H. Burer and Daniel
B. Wallace, "Was Junia Really an Apostle? A Re-examination of Rom 16.7,"
New Testament Studies 47 (2001): 76–91.

during the Council at Jerusalem held great sway (Acts 13:1–22). He may have been an apostle.

The apostle Paul also mentioned some of these other apostles in 1 Corinthians 15:1–8, when he listed Christ's resurrection appearances to various groups of people, as we saw above. In addition to Cephas [Peter] and the Twelve, "he appeared to more than five hundred brothers at one time, most of whom are still alive, though some have fallen asleep. Then he appeared to James and all the apostles."

It's clear that the phrase "all the apostles" in verse 7 does not refer to the Twelve and Paul, whom Paul names separately in the list. There must have been other apostles.

Ephesians 4:11 also mentions other apostles. This verse lists apostles as being among the other gifted leaders Christ gave to the church. And since Ephesians was written about AD 60—some thirty years after Jesus' resurrection—this letter indicates that the Lord continued to provide apostles to the churches in the region at this later date.

What are we to make of this? How could there be additional apostles, coming late to the scene, if Paul claimed to be the last apostle? The mystery increases because of the fact that Paul was the author of this letter!

The answer is that there were different types of apostles during the first era of the Christian church.[4] The word *apostle* had a somewhat flexible range of meaning in the early church. It could be compared to the English word *messenger*, which is used with some flexibility today. A messenger can be sent by a human individual, by an institution, or by God. The type of apostle one was—with the accompanying level of authority—was determined by the identity of the senders and the circumstances of the sending.

So, Christians in the early church understood that some apostles were sent out directly by Christ and exerted extraordinary authority to govern the church and oversee the writing of Scripture. They

---

[4] See I. Howard Marshall, "Apostle," in *New Dictionary of Theology*, ed. Sinclair B. Ferguson and David F. Wright, Master Reference Collection (Downers Grove, IL: InterVarsity Press, 1988), 40.

included the Twelve, Paul, and several apostles mentioned in 1 Corinthians 15:7 who had seen the resurrected Lord and bore a special relationship to him. We'll refer to this group as "apostles of Christ."

Christians during the Apostolic Age also understood that other apostles were not directly commissioned by Jesus, but were sent out by churches for special tasks. These other apostles had important roles in ministry, but they probably did not exercise great authority like the Twelve and Paul. Rather, they functioned during that era much as missionaries, church planters, and church representatives do today. We'll call this group "apostles of the churches."[5]

False Apostles

In addition to the types of genuine apostles there is another group known as "false apostles." These imposters were both numerous and influential in the early church.

False apostles claimed to be apostles of Christ—with authority equal to the Twelve and Paul—though they had not been sent by Christ. Paul spoke of false apostles who had infiltrated the church at Corinth, where they tried to usurp his status as an apostle.

> *For such men are false apostles, deceitful workmen, disguising themselves as apostles of Christ. And no wonder, for even Satan disguises himself as an angel of light. So it is no surprise if his servants, also, disguise themselves as servants of righteousness. Their end will correspond to their deeds.* (2 Cor. 11:13–15)

False apostles also attempted to infiltrate the church at Ephesus. In this they failed. We know this because Jesus spoke about it through the revelation he gave to the apostle John, recorded in the book of Revelation. In his revelation to John, Jesus praised the church at Ephesus for thwarting the false apostles: "I know your works, your toil and your patient endurance, and how you cannot bear with those who

---

[5]   This designation, "apostles of the churches," was used by the apostle Paul. See 2 Corinthians 8:23.

are evil, but have tested those who call themselves apostles and are not, and found them to be false" (Rev. 2:2).

How did the Ephesian Christians recognize the false apostles in their midst? They must have observed characteristics resembling those displayed by the false apostles at the church at Corinth. Those false apostles were motivated by money (2 Cor. 2:17). They were self-promoting (2 Cor. 4:5) and concerned with superficialities—like physical appearance and polished speaking skills—rather than true inner spirituality (2 Cor. 5:12; 10:10). They were arrogant, boasting that they were "super-apostles" (2 Cor. 11:5; 12:11). They deceptively twisted Scripture to serve their purposes (2 Cor. 4:2). Most alarmingly, they did not teach the truth about Christ and his saving work, but instead preached "another Jesus" and a "different gospel" (2 Cor. 11:4).

In addition, they falsely claimed they received visions and revelations from God. This explains why Paul felt the need to "boast"— contrary to his humble instincts—about his own visions and revelations, which, in contrast to theirs, were genuine (2 Cor. 12:1–4).

And they were unable to perform miracles. In contrast to these powerless apostles, Paul said of his own ministry to the Corinthians, "The signs of a true apostle were performed among you with utmost patience, with signs and wonders and mighty works" (2 Cor. 12:12).

These imitators attempted to convince the faithful. They made claims typical of the apostles, saying that they had received special knowledge from God and were able to exercise special powers. And *they did preach a gospel that included teachings about Jesus.* Hadn't the apostle Paul warned about teachers who would proclaim "another Jesus" than the true Jesus the apostles of Christ proclaimed (2 Cor. 11:4)? Some of the believers must have been vulnerable to the false apostles' teachings. This would account for Paul's own stern warning. They were not to mistake the Jesus preached by these false apostles with the Jesus who had genuinely and directly commissioned his own authentic apostles.

★★★

In summary, the best-known apostles in the Bible, the "apostles of Christ"—the Twelve and Paul—were sent directly by Christ to fulfill special missions in the early church and had unique roles to play. These roles included governance of the churches and oversight in the writing of Scripture. Other individuals are also referred to as apostles in the Bible, though these apostles did not perform the same roles or exercise the same level of authority as we see with the apostles of Christ. They were more like today's missionaries and church planters. They were "apostles of the churches." False apostles were also prevalent, and the Bible includes many warnings to stand guard against them.

4

NAR Apostles vs. Apostles in the Bible

We will now consider how NAR teachings on apostles hold up in comparison with what the Bible teaches.

Must Apostles Govern the Church?

In contrast to what NAR leaders teach, the Bible does not teach that apostles today must govern the church in the way the apostles of Christ governed. The three key passages frequently cited by NAR leaders fall short of supporting their teaching that apostles must govern.

Ephesians 4:11–13

NAR leaders lean heavily on Ephesians 4:11–13:

> And he gave the apostles, the prophets, the evangelists, the shepherds and teachers, to equip the saints for the work of ministry, for building up the body of Christ, until we all attain to the unity of the faith and of the knowledge of the Son of God, to mature manhood, to the measure of the stature of the fullness of Christ.

This passage says nothing about governing offices. It simply lists various types of gifted leaders God has given to build up the church. It doesn't state that these leaders must hold governing offices. In fact, it doesn't even list all the types of leaders God has given the church. For example, it says nothing about elders (also called overseers) or deacons, though these two types of leaders are clearly discussed in other passages of the Bible (1 Tim. 3:1–13; Titus 1:5–9). So, it's an incorrect interpretation of this passage to say that it teaches that the church must have five ongoing governing offices, including the offices of apostle and prophet.

Ephesians 2:20

Another passage used by NAR leaders is Ephesians 2:20:

> *[The church is] built on the foundation of the apostles and prophets, Christ Jesus himself being the cornerstone.*

As we pointed out with the previous passage, this verse says nothing about governing offices. Furthermore, it is speaking about the time period at the beginning of the church, when it was founded by first-century apostles and prophets. So it cannot properly be used to teach that there are ongoing offices of apostle and prophet.

1 Corinthians 12:28

The third favorite is 1 Corinthians 12:28:

> *And God has appointed in the church first apostles, second prophets, third teachers, then miracles, then gifts of healing, helping, administrating, and various kinds of tongues.*

Again, notice that this passage says nothing about governing offices; it only lists some of the types of leaders God has given to his church. The list includes not only apostles and prophets, but also other types of ministries like helping, administrating, and speaking in various kinds of tongues. No one we know of—not even NAR leaders—claims there should be governing offices of helping or speaking in tongues. So why claim that this verse teaches that apostles, prophets, and teachers hold a governing office, but those other gifted persons do not? There must be a good reason to treat items in the same list differently.

Many NAR leaders would say that apostles and prophets are treated differently because they're identified in the verse as "first" and "second." Yet apostles are not identified in this way because they are powerful figures in a hierarchical church government. Rather, they are so identified because their functions—proclaiming the gospel and speaking words that strengthen churches—are of fundamental importance. The teaching ministry of the church is crucial to the health of the church and the proper function of the other ministries.

WAS THE GOVERNING OFFICE OF APOSTLE TEMPORARY?

The governing office of apostle was temporary. There are at least three indications of this.

First, the twelve apostles had a unique role as companions of Jesus and eyewitnesses of Jesus' earthly ministry. With their passing, there would be no more living eyewitnesses with such authority, at liberty to add records of Jesus' life and teachings. This closes the door on the emergence of additional apostles who would claim to share in their unique office.

Second, Paul reasoned that he was the final apostle. For him, receiving a personal appearance from the resurrected Christ was a requirement for being a late-arriving apostle (1 Cor. 9:1). Since he was the last individual to whom the resurrected Lord appeared, he was the last to qualify for apostleship (1 Cor. 15:8).

Third, Scripture gives no instructions for appointing future apostles, and no indication that any should be recognized following the deaths of the apostles of Christ.[1] But Scripture does provide instructions for the appointment of elders and deacons (1 Tim. 3:1–13; Titus 1:5–9). If God intended for apostles to govern the church in the next and every later generation, as NAR leaders claim, then surely the authors of Scripture would have made this clear.[2]

---

[1]   Matthias was chosen to replace Judas after Judas betrayed Jesus and killed himself. But after the circle of twelve apostles was completed with Matthias, no attempt was made to replace any of the Twelve after their deaths.

[2]   NAR leaders teach that apostles were suppressed after the first couple of centuries. See, for example, C. Peter Wagner, *Changing Church* (Ventura, CA: Regal Books, 2006), 7.

Even those apostles who held a temporary office in church governance did not exert their authority beyond the local precincts of the church to govern the affairs of Christians working in various sectors of society, like business and government. The office of apostle was an office *for the church*. Those who filled this office did not have authority extending beyond the church. There is, then, no biblical support for the notion of what NAR leaders call workplace apostles. It may sound like a good idea. But it wasn't God's idea. He has, however, offered general guidance in Scripture for the conduct of all of life. We are to do all things, including our professional work, "as for the Lord" (Col. 3:23).

Is There Any Role in the Church Today for Apostles Who Do Not Govern?

There is a role in the church today for individuals who function, in some ways, as apostles, but who do not govern the church.

The apostle Paul clarifies this ongoing role in Ephesians 4:11–13, where he lists the types of gifted leaders God has given to build up the church. This passage—written some 30 years after Jesus' resurrection—speaks of the church in its ongoing structure, apparently for generations to come.

Recall that the word *apostles* carried a flexible range of meaning in the time the New Testament was written. It could refer to the apostles of Christ, whom he specially appointed and to whom he gave extraordinary authority for church governance. Or it could refer to those who were sent out by churches to act as missionaries and church planters but who did not hold official offices governing the church; that is, the apostles of the churches. If used in this second sense of the word—as referring to missionaries and church planters—then one could say that there are still apostles today.

But to avoid confusion, we think it best today to avoid use of the word apostle when referring to missionaries and church planters. In New Testament times, people would have realized that the word carried a flexible range of meaning. But applying it to people today—when most Christians think of apostles as having extraordinary authority, like the Twelve and Paul—is sure to cause confusion. Theologian Wayne Grudem (himself a charismatic) agrees with the wisdom of setting aside the title of apostle. "It is noteworthy," he says, "that no major leader in the history of the church—not Athanasius or Augustine, not Luther or Calvin, not Wesley or Whitefield—has taken to himself the title of 'apostle' or let himself be called an apostle."[3]

We think confusion is caused when church leaders today claim the mantle of apostle, even if they see themselves merely as evangelists or church planters. As we'll see in the next section, confusion lapses into dangerous error when a figure today claims to be an apostle after the fashion of Paul or the Twelve.

Testing NAR Apostles

NAR apostles do not claim merely to be missionaries and church planters. Rather, they claim to hold a formal office in church government, similar to the apostles of Christ. In our assessment, however, NAR leaders have failed to produce biblical support for their teaching that apostles today must govern the church. But even if they could provide the needed support, NAR apostles would still have to pass five biblical tests for being genuine apostles.

What are these tests? First, they must have quite literally seen the resurrected Lord. Second, they must have received a specific commission by Christ in the fashion of those first commissioned during the Apostolic Age. Third, they must perform miracles that witness to their authority as apostles of Christ. Fourth, any new teachings or practices they promote must be supported in Scripture. And, fifth, they must exhibit an exemplary quality of ministry and lives of the highest level of virtue and integrity. Let's consider each of these tests.

---

[3] Wayne Grudem, *Systematic Theology: An Introduction to Biblical Doctrine* (Grand Rapids, Zondervan, 1994), 911.

An Appearance from Christ

Seeing Jesus personally is something that many—but not all—NAR apostles claim to have experienced. Apostle Peter Wagner believes that a personal appearance from Christ should not serve as a litmus test for determining whether a person is truly an apostle.[4] Why not? This is curious. For Paul, having "seen Jesus our Lord" was a criterion for all apostles of Christ (see 1 Cor. 9:1). Why, then, are NAR apostles exempt? Wagner doesn't say. (He does maintain, however, that about twenty percent of the apostles he knows have seen Jesus personally.) Yet other prominent NAR apostles, such as Rick Joyner, do believe an appearance from Christ is a non-negotiable requirement for being an apostle.[5]

But it is not enough to claim to have seen Christ. If such a claim is to be believed, the claimant must demonstrate that the appearance occurred. How would one do that? In the case of the apostle Paul, others could provide testimony to back up his claim. Paul's traveling companions were on the scene when Christ appeared to him. They did not see Christ, but they saw the bright light and heard the sound of his voice. They also saw the powerful effect Christ's appearance had on Paul—how it blinded him for three days. After he appeared to Paul, Christ also appeared to another person, Ananias, in a vision and told him of his appearance to Paul. Ananias, then, could provide further testimony to substantiate Paul's claim. Also, and this is crucial, Paul took counsel with the apostles of Christ after a lengthy period of reflection and self-examination. Three years into his Christian life he went up to Jerusalem to see Peter—the acknowledged leader of the Twelve—and remained with him for fifteen days (Gal. 1:18). Paul sees this meeting as a validation of his own credentials as an apostle.

---

[4]   C. Peter Wagner, *Apostles Today: Biblical Government for Biblical Power* (Ventura, CA: Regal Books, 2006), 30–31.

[5]   Rick Joyner, *The Apostolic Ministry* (Wilkesboro, NC: MorningStar Publications, 2004), 78.

Evidently his time with Peter was critical for confirming Paul's status as an apostle. This was evidence that he was the real deal.

Paul's instantaneous, radical conversion—from a persecutor of the Christians to one of their most vocal leaders—suggested that he had a genuine encounter with Christ. Christ's appearance to Paul was not just an empty claim with no independent validation. Others could attest to it, and to the life-changing effects it had on him (Gal. 1:11–24).

NAR apostles cannot dismiss the requirement to have seen Christ. And if they truly have received an appearance from him, then others should be able to confirm it.[6] Surely God, who appointed no less than twelve official eyewitnesses to contribute to the writing of four separate Gospel accounts of Christ's life—and to vouch for Paul— would be as concerned to provide multiple voices of testimony to verify that a modern-day apostle had experienced a literal visitation from Jesus Christ.

A Specific Commission by Christ

An appearance from Christ, however, does not by itself make a person an apostle. According to Scripture, Jesus appeared after his resurrection to more than five hundred "brothers" at one time (1 Cor. 15: 6). Yet these individuals were not recognized as apostles, presumably because Jesus had not specifically appointed them as such.

Jesus explicitly commissioned the twelve apostles twice—both before and following his resurrection (Matt. 10:1–7 and Acts 1:8). When filling the apostolic office left vacant by Judas, the apostles submitted to the selection Christ made through the unusual device of casting of lots (Acts 1:24–26).

NAR leaders do teach that apostles are appointed directly by God. But they are publicly affirmed as apostles when they are commissioned into the office by other apostles. Thus, the appointment of a

---

[6] Not only should others be able to confirm an appearance from Christ, but these others also should be of comparable stature, as was Peter in the case of Paul. The logic of this situation would require an unbroken chain of apostolic officials going back to the original apostles.

NAR apostle by God isn't necessarily a public event that can be confirmed with outside validation, as when Christ appointed the Twelve and Paul. Past appointments by Christ were objective events allowing for public verification.

The appointment of NAR apostles by God seems very different from the appointments of the apostles of Christ. The unverifiable nature of NAR appointments may explain why they feel the need to hold public commissioning ceremonies to affirm that they are truly apostles.

In our view, a genuine apostle who shared the status of the apostles of Christ would be appointed specifically by Christ in a manner that allowed for outside confirmation of the event. There would be no need for a separate, public commissioning ceremony.

Performance of Miracles

Performing miracles is something that many, though perhaps not all, NAR apostles claim to have done. Wagner believes that working miraculous signs and wonders is not required of NAR apostles.[7] Again, this is curious. The apostle Paul distinguished himself from false apostles—those who were only pretending to be apostles—in part by his ability to work real miracles (2 Cor. 12:12).

So why are NAR apostles exempt from this requirement? Again, Wagner doesn't say.

Other prominent NAR leaders, such as Bill Hamon, do believe that miracles are required of all today's apostles.[8] And though Wagner does not believe miracles are required, he does claim that "almost" every apostle he knows has seen physical healings in their ministries.[9]

---

[7] Wagner, *Apostles Today*, 30–31.

[8] Bill Hamon, *Apostles, Prophets, and the Coming Moves of God: God's End-Time Plans for His Church and Planet Earth* (Santa Rosa Beach, FL: Destiny Image Publishers, 1997), 32–34.

[9] Wagner, *Apostles Today*, 31.

He adds, "but not many have seen mass healings through the casting of their shadow as did Peter (Acts 5:15)."

What should go without saying is that mere claims to have performed physical healings do nothing to support claims that a person is truly an apostle. Alleged miracles must be spectacular and they must be verifiable.

The miraculous signs performed by the Twelve and Paul were not easy to miss. Their awe-inspiring works included raising the dead and healing the paralyzed. Their miraculous powers were not limited to healing conditions that it would be difficult to verify, such as backaches or emotional pain. Furthermore, their miraculous signs were performed publicly so there would be no doubt they had occurred. No one was expected to settle for taking the apostles of Christ merely at their word.

Notice, we're not arguing against gifts of healing (1 Cor. 12:9) that may be used to cure backaches or emotional pain. Healings of these types of conditions certainly would bless those who experience them, even though they may not be as dramatic as healings of paralysis or blindness. Nor are we arguing that miracles of other types do not occur. Our point is simply that a miracle must be astonishing—as were those of the original apostles—if we are to be convinced that a modern-day apostle is among us.

We are also not arguing that all healings must be conducted publicly. Healings experienced in private settings may serve mainly for the benefit of the persons healed and not as miraculous signs for others. We suspect, in fact, that God does, in the typical case, heal in response to prayer.

Unlike these less dramatic and less verifiable types of healings, when an apostle claims to have performed a miraculous sign it should be impressive and it should be confirmed by evidence that can be publicly verified. Reliable eyewitness testimony and, if at all possible, medical documentation are reasonable requests regarding miraculous signs that are said to provide evidence for their claim to be special representatives of God.

Support in Scripture for Any New Teachings and Practices

Any new teachings and practices taught by NAR apostles must be supported in Scripture. Even the apostle Paul was not exempt from this criterion. When he brought new teachings to the Jews in Berea, they examined the Scripture to see if his teachings found support there (Acts 17:11) and determined that they did. The fact that even Paul, the great apostle, could only give new teachings if they had the support of Scripture shows how crucial this criterion is for testing today's apostles. It becomes even more crucial in light of Paul's warning about false apostles who disguise themselves as true apostles (2 Cor. 11:13).

Of course, Wagner says the new revelations taught by NAR apostles don't *contradict* Scripture: "The one major rule governing any new revelation from God is that it cannot contradict what has already been written in the Bible. It may supplement it, however."[10] This reflects a desire to uphold the authority of Scripture. But to say it is enough if NAR revelations do not *contradict* Scripture is setting the bar too low. The Wagner test is too weak. Any new revelation must reflect *continuity* with revelation that has already been given. We call this principle of essential continuity the Berean Principle. Something like this principle is implied in the way the Bereans tested Paul's preaching when he visited their synagogue. They were "examining the Scriptures daily to see if these things were so." And as a result, many believed (see Acts 17:10–12). The Bereans must have recognized in Paul's teaching some deep continuity with the Scriptures they had before them.

So how can you know if new revelation—like new truths revealed by NAR apostles and prophets—has the right kind of continuity with Scripture? How do you apply the Berean Principle? We suggest three criteria: extension, expectation, and expansion.

---

[10]   C. Peter Wagner, "The New Apostolic Reformation Is Not a Cult," *Charisma News*, August 24, 2011; accessed January 7, 2014, http://www.charismanews.com/opinion/31851-the-new-apostolic-reformation-is-not-a-cult.

Extension. First, new revelation cannot be *completely* new. It must be an extension of what has already been revealed. New revelation always extends our knowledge of God beyond what was known before. But it is always a recognizable extension of what has already been revealed. It doesn't come totally out of left field. This was true of Jesus when he fulfilled prophecies about the Messiah. For example, God revealed that he would work his plan of redemption through the descendants of Abraham (Gen. 3). Later, the revelation is extended when we learn that, of Abraham's two sons—Ishmael and Isaac—the plan of redemption would be worked through the descendants of Isaac (Gen. 21:12). Then we learn that, of Isaac's sons, redemption would be worked through the family line of Jacob (Gen. 28:14). On and on the original revelation is extended—through Judah, Jesse, and David—revealing additional individuals through whom the Messiah would descend. All this revelation is an extension of the original revelation given to Abraham.

Expectation. Second, any new revelation should also be anticipated or hinted at in what already has been revealed. In other words, there should be some trace of the old revelation in the new. For example, the Old Testament contains revelation about an individual that is "wounded for our transgressions" (Isa. 53:5). Thus, the New Testament revelation that Jesus died on the cross for our sins was hinted at in past revelation.

Expansion. Third, any new revelation should expand upon existing revelation. An inspection of what is new, for anyone already familiar with the old, will call to mind the old that is present in the new, where it is filled in with more details. The old revelation is fleshed out in the new. For example, in the Old Testament, we find words God told King David at his coronation: "You are my Son: today I have begotten you." God, at that time, was speaking to David, referring to David as his Son. Yet, this revelation about David in the Old Testament was expanded in the New Testament, where we learn that it also applies to Jesus: Jesus too was also declared to be God's Son (Rom. 1:4), but in a new and fuller way.

These are three criteria for evaluating any new revelation to see if it has continuity with revelation already given in Scripture. But the new truths taught by today's apostles and prophets do not meet these criteria. NAR revelation strikes out in a bold new direction. NAR leaders have pioneered a sweeping new theology without showing that it has any connection with existing revelation. Whatever connections they do make are generally without merit, depending as they do on verses stripped from their context and hastily interpreted as proof texts for their views.

So it is not enough for NAR leaders to claim that their new revelation doesn't *contradict* Scripture. This claim is too weak. The Wagner test defending NAR new truths is unacceptable. If apostles cannot link their new revelation claims to existing revelation, then it is safe to ignore their claims and it is potentially dangerous to embrace them.

Quality of Life and Ministry

A genuine apostle will have an exemplary quality of ministry and a distinctly virtuous character.[11] The fruit of an apostle's ministry, like that of the apostle Paul, will be people responding to the gospel and becoming true disciples of Jesus, reflected in lives changed by the work of the Holy Spirit (1 Cor. 9:12, 16–18; 15:1, 14; 2 Cor. 3:2–3; 1 Thess. 2:1–13).

Genuine apostles will also be willing to endure great suffering in fulfillment of their commissions, as did the apostle Paul (2 Cor. 1:5, 8-9; 11:23–28). They will not use methods that are deceitful or tamper with Scripture (2 Cor. 4:2). They will be motivated by sincerity (2 Cor. 1:12) and be marked by the character traits of self-sacrifice (1 Cor. 9:1–15, 19) and humility (2 Cor. 11:7).

It's noteworthy that character is a criterion Wagner considers absolutely indispensable in an apostle.[12] The one character trait he

---

[11] See Michael W. Austin and R. Douglas Geivett, eds., *Being Good: Christian Virtues for Everyday Life* (Grand Rapids: Eerdmans, 2012).

[12] Wagner, *Apostles Today*, 44–45.

describes at length is humility. But other tests are just as critical for evaluating alleged apostles.

In light of these several tests, how do NAR teachings about apostles fare? Screening their claims by multiple biblical criteria, NAR teachings about apostles fall short.

★★★

In summary, the Bible does not support the NAR teaching that apostles today must govern the church. Rather, it indicates that the governing office of apostle was temporary. There is, however, a place in the church today for people who function in some ways as certain types of first-century apostles—as missionaries and church planters. But no one today has the extraordinary authority or unique functions of the twelve apostles or of Paul. If individuals claim such authority, they must pass five biblical tests for genuine apostleship. As far as we can tell, many NAR leaders either disregard these tests or fail to present convincing evidence that they have passed these tests.

In the next chapter we explain NAR teachings about prophets.

5

NAR Prophets: The Secret Intelligence Agents

A prophet named Caleb was highly regarded by a number of churches in the Pacific Northwest and Canada. He was in demand wherever he went. At one particular city, his followers scheduled appointments with him to receive guidance on every imaginable issue, including business ventures, marriage advice, and ministry callings. In return, many supported him financially.

One married couple was so dependent on Caleb that they would fly him to their city—more than three thousand miles away—whenever they needed critical counsel. Acting on his advice about ten years ago, they cashed out their retirement savings for a business venture related to real estate. Caleb assured them that their investment would succeed. They would give of its profits to God. But shortly after his assurance, the housing market crashed. Now, nearly a decade later, the venture has failed and the family has been unable to secure a bank loan to meet expenses. The couple still regards Caleb as a true prophet, however, and believe he can help them uncover—and cast out—any demons thwarting their business.

The couple's faith in Caleb as a prophet begs the question, "Are there really prophets today?" That depends on who you ask. It also depends on what you mean by the term *prophets*.

In this chapter we will examine NAR teachings on prophets and, in chapter 6, review what the Bible teaches about prophets. In chapter 7, we evaluate NAR teachings on prophets in light of the Bible's teachings.

THE MAIN NAR TEACHING ON PROPHETS: THEY MUST GOVERN

As with the NAR teaching on apostles, the main NAR teaching about prophets—which sets NAR views apart from the views of other Christians—is that prophets must govern the church. Prophets, like apostles, must have a role in directing the church in an authoritative way. But while apostles are viewed as generals, the prophets are seen more as secret intelligence agents. They know God's secret thoughts and plans and can guide churches based on their inside information.

NAR prophets claim to hold a formal office in church government like the office of pastor or elder. But prophets have much more authority than pastors and elders. This is because they act as God's official mouthpieces, similar to Old Testament prophets like Moses and Jeremiah. When NAR prophets speak they can boldly declare, "Thus saith the Lord." To disobey the words of a NAR prophet is to disobey God. Also, prophets—unlike pastors and elders—often have authority over multiple churches.

In contrast to this extravagant NAR view of prophets, Protestant Christians typically do not believe that modern-day prophets must govern churches. Some of these Protestant Christians—known as cessationists—believe that prophets' roles ceased completely after Scripture was written.[1] They think there is no need for any new revelation given by prophets once God's written Word was completed.

Other Protestant Christians—including Pentecostals and charismatics—believe many people today have a gift of prophecy. This

---

[1]   The Protestant Reformers, notably Martin Luther and John Calvin, were, on the whole, cessationists, as was Jonathan Edwards. A benchmark book arguing for cessationism is B. B. Warfield's *Counterfeit Miracles* (New York: Charles Scribner's Sons, 1918; repr., Charleston, SC: Nabu Press, 2010). Contemporary cessationist scholars include John MacArthur, O. Palmer Robertson, and Richard B. Gaffin Jr. For multiple perspectives by different authors, see Wayne A. Grudem, ed., *Are Miraculous Gifts for Today? Four Views* (Grand Rapids, MI: Zondervan, 1996); and Daniel B. Wallace and M. James Sawyer, eds., *Who's Afraid of the Holy Spirit? An Investigation into the Ministry of the Spirit of God Today* (Dallas, TX: Biblical Studies Press, 2005).

does involve receiving revelation from God. These church prophets, as they are called, speak words that strengthen, encourage, and comfort individual Christians and local churches. But they don't have an official position in church government as NAR prophets do.

How do NAR prophets wield their authority to govern churches?

They are usually invited to a local church by a pastor. The prophet will then deliver words of guidance, instruction, rebuke, judgment, and revelation, "whatever Christ chooses to speak for the purifying and perfecting of His Church," according to prophet-apostle Bill Hamon.[2] For example, a prophet may reveal a change of direction for a church, a change in leadership, or whether a church is fulfilling God's particular purpose for it.

But why would pastors invite prophets to their churches? Because this practice, called receiving a prophet, is important in NAR. A church is expected to accept the words of a prophet as the very words of God. By doing so, people in NAR believe they will be blessed and rewarded by God. They base this belief on their understanding of Matthew 10:41: "The one who receives a prophet because he is a prophet will receive a prophet's reward."

Failure to receive a prophet results in loss of reward. But something even worse—God's judgment—will come to those who dare to challenge a prophet. Many NAR leaders teach that God gives a stern warning about speaking against prophets in Psalm 105:15: "Touch not my anointed ones, do my prophets no harm!" As Bill Hamon says, "He who curses one of God's true prophets incurs the curse of God."[3]

Pastors can also receive prophets into their churches by joining an apostolic network. Since apostles and prophets are supposed to work together, many apostolic networks are governed by apostle-prophet teams, such as Harvest International Ministry (HIM), an apostolic network made up of more than 20,000 churches in fifty nations and

---

[2] Bill Hamon, *Prophets and Personal Prophecy: God's Prophetic Voice Today* (Shippensburg, PA: Destiny Image Publishers, 2001), 36.

[3] Ibid., 8.

directed by the apostle Ché Ahn and the prophet James Goll. Goll's revelations provide direction for pastors in the entire network of 20,000 churches.

APOSTOLIC COUNCIL OF PROPHETIC ELDERS

Many well-known prophets in NAR are members of the Apostolic Council of Prophetic Elders, formed in 1999. This council meets together before the start of each year to pray and receive revelation from God. They compile the revelations they receive and release an annual "Word of the Lord," which is published by influential media organizations, including *Charisma* magazine. Predictions released through these "Word of the Lord" reports over the years include people miraculously rising from the dead, the toppling of Iran's nuclear power, and an increase of "holiness" in universities (including surprising departures of "radical leftist professors").[a]

Membership is by invitation only and includes approximately twenty to twenty-five persons at any given time. The full membership list is no longer made public, but individuals who have been identified as either present or former members include:

- Cindy Jacobs (the convening apostle) and Mike Jacobs, both of Generals International;
- C. Peter Wagner of Global Spheres with his wife, Doris Wagner;
- Bill Hamon of Christian International;
- Chuck Pierce of Global Spheres;
- Steve Shultz of The Elijah List;
- Mary Glazier of Windwalkers International;
- Mike Bickle of the International House of Prayer;
- Paul Cain (honorary member) of Paul Cain Ministries;
- Sharon Stone of Christian International Europe;
- Harry Jackson of Hope Christian Church in Beltsville, Maryland;
- Rick Ridings of Succat Hallel in Jerusalem;
- John and Paula Sandford of Elijah House;
- Michael Schiffman of Chevra USA;
- Jean Steffenson of Native American Resource Network;
- Dominic Yeo of Trinity Christian Centre in Singapore;
- Elizabeth Alves, an author and former long-time board member of Aglow International;

- Gwen Shaw of End-Time Handmaidens and Servants International;
- Wesley and Stacey Campbell of Revival Now Ministries;
- David McCracken of David MacCracken Ministries;
- Héctor Torres of Hispanic International Ministries;
- Barbara Wentroble of International Breakthrough Ministries;
- Bart Pierce of Rock City Church in Baltimore, Maryland;
- Barbara Yoder of Shekinah Regional Apostolic Center in Ann Arbor, Michigan;
- Kim Clement of Kim Clement Center;
- Paul Keith Davis of White Dove Ministries;
- Lou Engle of The Call;
- James Goll of Encounters Network;
- Jim Laffoon of King's Park International Church in Durham, North Carolina;
- Ong Sek Leang of Metro Tabernacle in Malaysia;
- Joseph Garlington of Covenant Church of Pittsburgh in Pennsylvania;
- Ernest Gentile of Christian Community Church in San Jose, California;
- Dutch Sheets of Dutch Sheets Ministries; and
- Tommy Tenny of GodChasers Network.[b]

a. See Steve Shultz, "2003 Word of the Lord—Apostolic Council of Prophetic Elders," The Elijah List, February 24, 2003; accessed February 25, 2014, https://www.elijahlist.com/words/display_word.html?ID=1409; C. Peter Wagner, Cindy Jacobs et al., "Word of the Lord for 2007—Released through the Apostolic Council of Prophetic Elders," The Elijah List, November 1, 2006; accessed February 25, 2014, http://www.elijahlist.com/words/display_word/4655; "ACPE Word of the Lord for 2014," Generals News, January 29, 2014, Generals International; accessed May 5, 2014, http://www.generals.org/news/single-view/article/acpe-word-of-the-lord-for-2014.

b. These names are listed in prefaces to the Apostolic Council of Prophetic Elders "Word of the Lord" documents that have been published by The Elijah List through the years. See Steve Shultz, "2003 Word of the Lord—Apostolic Council of Prophetic Elders"; Wagner, Jacobs et al., "Word of the Lord for 2007—Released Through the Apostolic Council of Prophetic Elders."

Key Bible Passages Used
to Defend NAR Teaching on Prophets

The three passages NAR leaders usually cite to defend the teaching that prophets must govern the church are the same passages used to defend the teaching that apostles must govern: Ephesians 4:11–13, Ephesians 2:20, and 1 Corinthians 12:28. We've already explained and evaluated the NAR understandings of these passages. Here we'll simply mention briefly another verse NAR leaders point to to defend their teachings about prophets, Amos 3:7:

> For the LORD God does nothing
> without revealing his secret
> to his servants the prophets.

NAR leaders say this verse shows that prophets must always govern the church because they are the ones to whom God reveals his "secrets."

NAR leaders also make another argument from Scripture. They claim that several Old Testament prophets had key functions in governing the nation of Israel, including Moses, Samuel, and David.[4] Therefore, prophets in the New Testament must also have governed the church.

We'll evaluate the NAR understandings of these passages in chapter 7.

Other Things NAR Prophets Do

As we look at other things NAR prophets do outside local churches, we'll focus on the teachings of Bill Hamon, the founder of Christian International Ministries Network in Santa Rosa Beach, Florida. We focus on Hamon's teachings because he is an extremely influential prophet in NAR. He is often called the father of the modern prophetic movement and has been featured as a leading prophet in

---

[4] Bill Hamon, *Prophets and the Prophetic Movement: God's Prophetic Move Today* (Shippensburg, PA: Destiny Image Publishers, 2001), 158–59.

Charisma magazine.[5] His books are endorsed by well-known NAR leaders, including Peter Wagner, Cindy Jacobs, and David Cannistraci. When explaining Hamon's views we do not mean to imply that every leader associated with NAR shares all his views. But we have observed similarities between many of his views and those of other leaders in NAR.

According to Hamon, in addition to governing local churches, prophets have been authorized by God to do the following things for individuals, nations, and the global church.

Prophesying to individuals

Prophets who hold the office can give specific, directive words to individuals regarding their personal lives. In contrast, people who have only the spiritual gift of prophecy but have not been formally ordained to the office by a prophetic presbytery are discouraged from giving directive prophecies to individuals.[6]

Specific things prophets do for individuals include:[7]

- revealing, imparting, and activating (or releasing) spiritual gifts while laying their hands on an individual;
- revealing and confirming those with a call to one of the fivefold ministry offices (apostle, prophet, evangelist, pastor, or teacher);

---

[5]   The phrase "prophetic movement" refers to the movement that began in independent charismatic churches in the 1980s to restore prophets to the church.

[6]   A prophetic presbytery is a group of two or more prophets, sometimes called prophetic ministers, whose functions include the formal ordination of individuals to the fivefold ministry offices (apostle, prophet, evangelist, pastor, and teacher). See Hamon, *Prophets and Personal Prophecy*, 38–39; Bill Hamon, *Apostles, Prophets, and the Coming Moves of God: God's End-Time Plans for His Church and Planet Earth* (Santa Rosa Beach, FL: Destiny Image Publishers, 1997), 283.

[7]   These functions are identified in Hamon, *Prophets and Personal Prophecy*, 3, 14–15, 23, 24, 53, 81, 131–32.

- revealing God's personal will to individuals on major life decisions that are not addressed directly in Scripture, including whom to marry, which business decisions to make, and where to live;
- confirming what God has already told an individual;
- giving prophecies that result in physical healing; and
- identifying the root causes of psychiatric and psychological problems, resulting in the immediate inner healing of individuals.

Prophesying to nations

Prophets to nations—men and women like Bill Hamon and Cindy Jacobs—will have an increasingly critical role in the last days, according to NAR leaders. Hamon says, "Whole nations have arisen or fallen based on their response to God's word through His prophets."[8]

Specific things prophets do for nations include:[9]

- identifying the high-ranking demons that rule over nations, then leading spiritual warfare to destroy those demons;
- giving national leaders prophecies for their nations;
- accurately predicting earthquakes, tidal waves, and other catastrophes of nature,
- instilling the fear of God in people and turning entire nations to God;
- speaking into existence the plagues of the book of Revelation that will torment God's enemies in the last days; and
- confronting all false religious groups that practice supernatural spirit communication, including witches, occultists, spiritualists, New Agers, and Satan worshipers.[10]

---

[8]   Hamon, *Prophets and the Prophetic Movement*, 178.

[9]   The first four functions in this list are identified in Hamon, *Apostles, Prophets, and the Coming Moves of God*, 9–10, 116–17, 139, 232.

[10]   Hamon, *Prophets and the Prophetic Movement*, 85.

Prophesying to the global church

In addition to prophesying to individual churches or to local churches in a specific apostolic network, some prophets serve as prophets
to the entire church worldwide. These prophets claim that God has
revealed to them new truths—also commonly referred to as present
truth—for the entire church. The truths are often presented as strategies the church needs for it to advance God's kingdom on earth.

Even though they are called new truths, Hamon says they are not
actually new. Instead, they are "restored truths." These are teachings
and practices that were supposedly known and understood by early
Christians but were lost during the so-called Dark Ages of the church.

How are truths being restored by today's prophets? Through prophetic illumination of the Scripture, according to Hamon. Prophetic
illumination is when God gives a prophet supernatural insight into
the correct interpretation and application of a specific passage of
Scripture. It is like a light going on—suddenly the church develops
an understanding of a specific verse, through a prophet, that it did not
have prior to that time. Hamon says that the proper understandings
of certain Scriptures are "hidden from the eyes of men" until God's
time for that truth to be restored.[11] For example, he claims that it was
through prophetic illumination of Ephesians 2:8–9 that Martin Luther, the great leader of the Protestant Reformation, discovered the
truth that salvation is by faith alone.[12]

A key verse of Scripture used by NAR leaders to support the
idea that God has revealed new truths to NAR prophets is Ephesians
3:4–5: "When you read this, you can perceive my insight into the
mystery of Christ, which was not made known to the sons of men
in other generations as it has now been revealed to his holy apostles
and prophets by the Spirit." Hamon says the apostle Paul teaches here
that both apostles and prophets are given the revelation ministry for

---

[11]   Hamon, *Prophets and Personal Prophecy*, 10.

[12]   Ibid., 11.

the church.[13] But while apostles hear from God, they generally do not hear from him as clearly as prophets do, according to NAR leaders. So prophets are indispensable for revealing new truths to the church. It is then the task of the apostles to use their authority to implement (or apply) in churches the new/restored truths that have been revealed by the prophets.[14]

What are the new truths the prophets have revealed? They include numerous NAR teachings and practices, such as strategic-level spiritual warfare, the Seven Mountain Mandate, and 24/7 prayer. Hamon teaches that all the new truths that have been revealed by prophets must be embraced by Christians so they don't miss out on what God wants to do through them and the church to advance his kingdom.[15]

The idea that contemporary prophets can reveal new truths for the global church is an astounding claim. We evaluate this claim in chapter 7.

★★★

In summary, prophets in NAR are viewed as spiritual secret intelligence agents who know the secret thoughts and plans of God. NAR leaders teach that all churches and individual Christians must submit to prophets' leadership so they can advance God's kingdom and receive his blessing and reward. Those who challenge the prophets face God's judgment.

In the next chapter, we review what the Bible teaches about prophets.

---

[13]   Ibid., 11.

[14]   C. Peter Wagner, *Changing Church* (Ventura, CA: Regal Books, 2004), 13–14.

[15]   Bill Hamon, *The Day of the Saints: Equipping Believers for Their Revolutionary Role in Ministry* (Shippensburg, PA: Destiny Image Publishers, 2002), 49.

6

Prophets in the Bible: A Close Look

Now that we've looked at NAR teachings on prophets, we'll review what the Bible teaches about them.

OLD TESTAMENT PROPHETS

Most of the Bible's best-known prophets are found in the Old Testament—men like miracle-working Moses, fiery Elijah, and weeping Jeremiah.

Prophets' Messages

Throughout Israel's history, God sent prophets to guide his chosen nation and give his people instruction, correction, warnings of judgment, and consolation. These prophets received their messages from God in diverse ways—through visions and dreams, from angelic messengers, and by hearing his audible voice.

The prophets shared common messages. Their major message was a call for the Israelites to keep the Mosaic covenant. For this reason, they've been referred to as "covenant enforcers."[1]

The Mosaic covenant was a special relationship God arranged with Israel. God promised to make Israel into a "kingdom of priests" that would serve as a light to the rest of the nations (Exod. 19:5–6). If the Israelites obeyed the laws God revealed to them through the prophet Moses, then they would reflect God's righteousness and justice, and they would channel God's presence and blessings to the entire world.

---

[1]   Philip S. Johnston, ed., *The IVP Introduction to the Bible* (Downers Grove, IL: InterVarsity Press, 2006), 38, 118.

To help the Israelites remain faithful to the covenant, God promised to raise up a series of prophets, culminating in a specific great prophet like Moses (Deut. 18:15).[2] The message of these prophets—a call to covenant faithfulness—is summarized by the unknown author of 1 and 2 Kings:

> Yet the LORD warned Israel and Judah by every prophet and every seer, saying, "Turn from your evil ways and keep my commandments and my statutes, in accordance with all the Law that I commanded your fathers, and that I sent to you by my servants the prophets." (2 Kings 17:13)

The Israelites, however, did not heed this message. So the prophets foretold the coming of a new covenant (Jer. 31:31–34) and a Messiah who would initiate that covenant (Heb. 12:24). The coming of the Messiah was the ultimate message of the Old Testament prophets. Jesus said as much when he told his disciples:

> "O foolish ones, and slow of heart to believe all that the prophets have spoken! Was it not necessary that the Christ should suffer these things and enter into his glory?" And beginning with Moses and all the Prophets, he interpreted to them in all the Scriptures the things concerning himself. (Luke 24:25–27)

Prophets' Backgrounds

Certain Old Testament prophets stand out, like Moses and Elijah. But there also were many more lesser-known prophets, some of them unnamed (Judg. 6:7–10; 1 Sam. 2:27–36; 1 Kings 13:1–3). Some prophets' words were not even recorded in Scripture and their books have been lost, such as Iddo and Ahijah the Shilonite (2 Chron. 9:29). Others prophesied only once, like the seventy elders appointed to assist Moses (Num. 11:24–25).

---

[2] Many Old Testament scholars see in this verse a promise that after Moses died, God would raise up a series of successive prophets. At the same time, they also see it—in light of the larger passage of Deut. 18:15–19—as a prediction of the coming of a specific great prophet like Moses. For this reason, many Israelites through the centuries were awaiting the arrival of this great prophet.

Prophets came from very different backgrounds. Amos was a shepherd, Jeremiah a priest, and Isaiah a royal court official. Women as well as men were prophets, including Miriam, Deborah, and Huldah.

Prophets' Functions

Guiding

Prophets were often consulted by Israel's leaders as they sought divine guidance on national matters, including war plans (1 Kings 22:5). King David consulted Nathan about his plans to build the temple (2 Sam. 7:1–7). King Jehoram asked Elisha if he should kill an army of captured Aramean soldiers (2 Kings 6:21–22).

Kings received most of the prophetic guidance in the Old Testament. But prophets also guided private citizens about personal matters. Before Saul was king he sought out a prophet to help him locate his father's lost donkeys (1 Sam. 9:6–10). His servant's suggestion to seek out a prophet indicates that this was a common custom.

Prophesying to Other Nations

A prophet's ministry didn't always stop at the borders of Israel. Prophets often pronounced judgments on other nations (Isaiah 13–23). Some were actually sent by God to other nations. Jonah was sent to the Assyrian city of Nineveh to warn its people of impending judgment. And Jeremiah was appointed to be a prophet to the nations (Jer. 1:5).

Receiving Revelation

Old Testament prophets were given revelation, which was preserved in Scripture. The Major Prophets—including Isaiah, Jeremiah, and Ezekiel—as well as the twelve Minor Prophets—including Hosea, Joel, and Amos— spoke divinely inspired messages that were written down in books. And the prophet Moses is traditionally regarded as the author of the Pentateuch, the first five books of the Old Testament.

Interceding with God

Prophets made intercession with God on behalf of individuals and the nation of Israel. For example, when the Israelites sinned by asking for a king, they asked Samuel to pray for their forgiveness so that God would not smite them (1 Sam. 12:19). And Moses' prayers influenced God to relent from destroying the Israelites in the desert (Exod. 32:10–33:17).

Worshipping

Prophets also contributed to Israel's worship. Some Levites, while serving at the temple, delivered spontaneous prophetic messages that caused the Israelites to worship God (2 Chron. 20:14–17). A number of the Levites' oracles came to be included in the book of Psalms, including Psalms 39, 50, 62, and 73 through 83. Some Levites prophesied in the form of song (1 Chron. 25:1–6), including Miriam (Num. 15:20–21). A group of prophets prophesied while accompanied by musical instruments (1 Sam. 10:5).

Prophetic Companies

The Old Testament also mentions prophetic companies, called sons of the prophets, whose functions aren't fully known. These companies were sometimes very large, with more than one hundred members (1 Kings 18:4). They were based at specific locations, including Bethel, Jericho, and Gilgal. They often served under a master prophet, like Elisha (2 Kings 4:1, 38; 6:1; 9:1), yet their own words were also authoritative. They're shown pronouncing judgment on Israel's kings (1 Kings 20:35–42), anointing kings (2 Kings 9:1–13), and predicting future events (2 Kings 2:3, 5).

In short, Old Testament prophets called the Israelites to covenant faithfulness and proclaimed a new covenant. Their functions included prophetically guiding kings and private individuals, prophesying to other nations, and receiving revelation. They also interceded with God on behalf of the Israelites, contributed to Israel's worship, and served in prophetic companies.

NEW TESTAMENT PROPHETS

When people think of prophets, they most often think of the great Old Testament prophets like Moses and Elijah. Yet many persons are also identified as prophets in the New Testament; some are not called prophets, but only described as prophesying. These people include John the Baptist, Elizabeth and Zechariah, Mary, Simeon, Anna, Jesus of Nazareth, those present at Pentecost, prophets at the church in Antioch, Judas and Silas, Agabus, the four daughters of Philip, prophets at the church in Corinth, and the "two witnesses" in the book of Revelation.

In addition, Paul, Peter, and John received special revelation from God. John received an entire book of prophecy, the book of Revelation. For this reason, some scholars conclude that these three apostles were both apostles and prophets.

Prophets' Message

Prophets in the New Testament, ministering under the New Covenant, didn't call people to obey the Mosaic covenant. They did, however, agree with the Old Testament prophets about the same ultimate message—the message of the Messiah. Jesus Christ was proclaimed by the first prophet of New Testament history, John the Baptist, and the last living apostle, John.

The apostle John confirmed that Jesus was the ultimate message of all the Bible's prophets, from both the Old Testament and the New, when he said that all prophecy points to Jesus: "For the testimony of Jesus is the spirit of prophecy" (Rev. 19:10).

Prophets' Purpose and Functions

The main purpose of New Testament prophets was to edify (that is, to build up) the church. According to Paul, building up the church was the purpose of all spiritual gifts, including the gift of prophecy (1 Cor. 12:7; 14:3–5, 12, 26). In Ephesians, prophets are listed among the types of gifted leaders God has provided for "building up the body of Christ" (Eph. 4:11–12). To edify the church, New Testament prophets did various things.

Receiving Revelation

We already noted that Paul, Peter, and John received revelation, which was written down in Scripture.

Guiding the Early Church

Prophets' revelation guided the growth of the early church. This is reflected in the activity of prophets at critical junctures in the book of Acts. Prophets at the church in Antioch revealed that God had chosen Barnabas and Paul for a special mission to the Gentiles (Acts 13:1–3). Two other prophets, Judas and Silas, traveled with Paul and Barnabas to Antioch, where they delivered the letter containing the decision made by the Council at Jerusalem (Acts 15:22, 32). While there, these two prophets spoke words that "encouraged and strengthened the brothers" in that particular church. Agabus predicted a famine that took place during the reign of the Roman emperor Claudius. His prophecy prompted the Christians at Antioch to send relief to the church at Jerusalem so the church could survive (Acts 11:28–30).

Prophesying in Church Meetings

Prophets were active at the church in Corinth, where they contributed prophecies during worship meetings. Paul advised the church to allow two or three prophets to give revelations "so that all may learn and all be encouraged" (1 Cor. 14:31). Though the wording of their prophecies isn't told, we know from this last verse that it included words of teaching and exhortation. And from 1 Corinthians 14:3 we know that "one who prophesies speaks to people for their upbuilding and encouragement and consolation."

Worshipping

Worship was a function of New Testament prophets, just as it was for prophets in the Old Testament. At Pentecost, those who prophesied spoke of "the mighty works of God" (Acts 2:11). And others in the New Testament delivered prophetically inspired words of praise similar to the inspired words of the Levites in the Old Testament, including Elizabeth (Luke 1:41–45), Mary (Luke 1:46–55), Zechariah (Luke 1:67–79), and Simeon (Luke 2:28–32).

Evangelism

Prophets also had an indirect function related to evangelism. Usually, their prophecies were for believers (1 Cor. 14:22). Yet prophecies could occasionally speak to unbelievers who came into the Christians' church meetings, thereby exposing the secrets of their hearts and causing them to worship God (1 Cor. 14:24–25).

Revealing Ministry Callings or Spiritual Gifting

In Paul's letters to Timothy, we learn that prophecies were given to Timothy at the time when Paul and the elders at the church in Ephesus laid their hands on him (1 Tim. 1:18; 4:14; 2 Tim. 1:6). Many scholars believe the event in view is Timothy's ordination to ministry and that the prophecies revealed God's call on his life or the specific spiritual gifts God had given him.

In short, many people are identified as prophets in the New Testament. Their main purpose was to build up the church, and their activities included receiving revelation, guiding the early church, prophesying in church meetings, worshipping, evangelism, and revealing ministry callings or spiritual gifting.

A Function Not Performed By New Testament Prophets

New Testament prophets apparently did not share a function that was typical of some Old Testament prophets. With two notable exceptions, New Testament prophets were never sent to prophesy to nations. The exceptions are John the Baptist and Jesus. Both were sent to the people of Israel, which, despite Roman rule, maintained a national identity. But prophets, following Pentecost, operated mostly within local churches, traveling occasionally to deliver prophecies to other Christians, as Agabus did with Paul. These prophets didn't pronounce judgments on nations.

After John and Jesus, the next time we see prophets declaring judgments on nations is in the book of Revelation, with the two witnesses who strike the earth with plagues (Rev. 11:6).[3] But these two witnesses won't appear until just before Christ's return, according to those scholars who believe that the book of Revelation foretells future events.[4]

FALSE PROPHETS

Genuine prophets are not the only prophets found in the pages of the Bible. There are also many false prophets.

In the Old Testament, false prophets include pagan prophets claiming to speak on behalf of pagan gods, such as the four hundred fifty prophets of Baal and the four hundred prophets of Asherah who served King Ahab and Queen Jezebel of Israel (1 Kings 18:19–20). In addition, there were false prophets from Israel who claimed to speak on behalf of the true God. They included Zedekiah and the four hundred prophets with him (1 Kings 22:5–12). Other unnamed false prophets of Israel were condemned by Isaiah (Isa. 28:7–13), Jeremiah (Jer. 23:9–40), Ezekiel (Ezekiel 13), and Micah (Mic. 3:5–12).

False prophets can also be found in the New Testament. Jesus specifically warned about false prophets when he said: "Beware of the false prophets, who come to you in sheep's clothing, but inwardly are ravenous wolves" (Matt. 7:15). He also warned that false prophets would be numerous: "Many false prophets will arise and will mislead many" (Matt. 24:11). And he said they would perform deceptive

---

[3] Bob DeWaay, "John the Baptist and Prophets to Nations," *Critical Issues Commentary*, Issue 67 (Nov./Dec. 2001); accessed August 30, 2014, http://www.cicministry.org/commentary/issue67.htm.

[4] Some scholars believe that most of the events in the book of Revelation have already transpired during the first century.

miracles to make it seem like they were actually true prophets. "For false Christs and false prophets will arise and will show great signs and wonders, so as to mislead, if possible, even the elect" (Matt. 24:24).

False prophets specifically identified in the New Testament are Elymas the magician (Acts 13:6–8), a woman called "Jezebel" (Rev. 2:20), and a miracle-working false prophet (Rev. 13:11–18; 16:13–14). Though only a few false prophets are identified specifically, there were many operating in the early church. Near the end of his life, the apostle John warned Christians that "many false prophets have gone out into the world" (1 John 4:1).

★★★

In summary, many genuine prophets can be found in the Bible in both the Old and New Testaments. We'll call them prophets of God. These prophets of God had numerous functions, though prophets in the New Testament generally didn't act as prophets to the nations, as did some Old Testament prophets. Many false prophets are also found in the Bible; we find multiple warnings to be alert to their presence.

7

NAR Prophets vs. Prophets in the Bible

We'll now consider how NAR teachings on prophets compare with the Bible's teachings.

MUST PROPHETS GOVERN THE CHURCH?

The Bible does not support the teaching that prophets today must govern the church. In chapter 4 we showed how the three key passages that NAR leaders frequently cite—Ephesians 4:11–13, Ephesians 2:20, and 1 Corinthians 12:28—do not support this teaching. There simply is no evidence that New Testament prophets held governing offices in the early churches. Other than the apostles of Christ, who held an exclusive office, the only two church offices clearly seen in the New Testament are elders (also called overseers) and deacons (1 Tim. 3:1–13; Titus 1:5–9). But if God intended that prophets should rule churches, as NAR leaders claim, then why isn't this clearly taught in Scripture? Given the Bible's silence on the topic, there's no reason to believe that prophets in the New Testament governed.

What about Old Testament prophets? Did they govern? NAR leaders say they did. Bill Hamon claims several Old Testament prophets had governing offices in Israel, like Samuel, who was a judge, and David, who was a king.[1] He concludes that prophets must have held governing offices in the New Testament church as well.

---

[1]   Bill Hamon, *Prophets and the Prophetic Movement: God's Prophetic Move Today* (Shippensburg, PA: Destiny Image Publishers, 2001), 158–59.

It's doubtful that Old Testament prophets governed the nation of Israel. It's true that some prophets also played national leadership roles. But it is going too far to claim that prophets held formal governing offices simply by virtue of their being prophets. In fact, once the nation of Israel was established, it was not led by prophets, but rather by judges and kings. While some of those judges and kings may also have been prophets, or at times spoken prophetically (as with Samuel and David), their authority to govern stemmed from their offices as judges and kings, not from their roles as prophets. Rather than governing, Old Testament prophets offered guidance to those who did govern. For example, the prophet Nathan served as an adviser to King David.

Another passage favored by NAR leaders and used to defend their teaching that prophets always must govern the church is Amos 3:7. This verse does show that God shares his perspective on world events with his prophets. Indeed, many of those perspectives have been recorded in Scripture. But this verse doesn't teach that prophets must govern. This should seem obvious, since Amos himself did not have any governing position. He wasn't even a spiritual leader in Israel. Rather, he was a mere shepherd (Amos 1:1).[2] So this verse shouldn't be used by NAR leaders to teach that prophets must govern.

ARE PROPHETS AUTHORIZED TO PROPHESY TO INDIVIDUALS?

The answer to this question depends on what is meant by prophesying to individuals. If the question is whether prophets are able to speak words inspired by God that strengthen, encourage, and comfort individual Christians, the answer may be yes. This will be true for anyone who believes that the spiritual gift of prophecy still operates in the church.

Yet many NAR leaders go further than this. NAR prophets not only speak words that strengthen, encourage, and comfort Christians.

---

[2] Some scholars think Amos may have been more of a businessman who bred sheep. In either case, he was not part of a spiritual governing elite.

Their prophecies also include the revealing of individuals' spiritual gifts and ministries and guidance for them in major life decisions.

It's true that prophecies were given to Timothy, and these seemed to involve his ministry calling or spiritual gifts (1 Tim. 1:18; 4:14; 2 Tim. 1:6). But this single instance is not enough to support a regular practice of prophets revealing callings and gifts. And there are no instances in the New Testament of a person receiving direction from a prophet about major life decisions, such as whom to marry or where to live.

In our view, such practices can be dangerous, especially in NAR. This is because NAR prophets claim to hold a formal church office with extraordinary authority. When a NAR prophet prophesies to an individual, that prophet's words will be seen as carrying greater authority than the words of a person who has only the spiritual gift of prophecy. It's always prudent to seek wise counsel about major life decisions from spiritually mature believers. But it's presumptuous for any counselor to declare God's specific will for a person beyond what is commanded in Scripture.[3]

Consider the couple who learned, during an ultrasound ten years ago, that their unborn baby daughter had several heart defects and other problems. Following the diagnoses, they were assured several times—by different family members and friends who claimed to have a prophetic gifting—that God was going to heal their baby. One man told them he had a vision of their unborn daughter running around a tent meeting, indicating that their baby would grow up to be a healthy little girl. But when the baby died just twenty-two hours after her birth, the mother, Carrie, was shocked because she thought healing had been guaranteed. Until the day of the baby's funeral, Carrie firmly believed that her child would return from the dead. She felt like God had failed her. If this mother could suffer such pain

---

[3] We agree with the view of decision-making presented by Garry Friesen in his book written with J. Robin Maxson, *Decision Making and the Will of God: A Biblical Alternative to the Traditional View* (Colorado Springs, CO: Multnomah Books, 1984, rev. 2004).

from the false promises of people who claimed to have a prophetic gifting, how much more devastating would be those same promises coming from the mouth of someone who called himself a prophet and claimed to hold a formal office.

Because of the extraordinary authority attached to the words of a NAR prophet, one danger is that people in NAR will become overly dependent on those prophets, being fearful to make any major life decision without first receiving guidance from a prophet.

Another danger is that people will obey the words of a NAR prophet as they would the words of God. This is only to be expected when a prophet claims to be speaking for God and people unwisely believe those claims.

Several years ago, Karen chose not to obey the words of a prophet named Caleb. Caleb advised Karen to forget about her financial debt and return to the mission field where her heart was leading her. He assured her that, if she did go back to the mission field, then God would take care of her debt and would give her every other thing her heart desired. But Karen's common sense and biblical wisdom told her the prophet's advice was not wise and that she should not be strapped down by debt when she went overseas.

In contrast to Karen, a married couple—the one mentioned at the start of chapter five—did obey this particular prophet's counsel to them. They cashed out their retirement savings to start a real estate venture. Yet to this day—nearly a decade later—they have nothing to show for the venture except a large, mostly vacant dirt lot. This is the type of harm that can occur to people who treat the words of a prophet as the words of God.

Do Prophets Today Prophesy to Nations?

It doesn't seem likely that prophesying to nations is part of the job description of prophets today.

After Pentecost, there is not a single example of a New Testament prophet advising civil rulers or pronouncing judgments on nations.

Perhaps this is because they were busy preaching the gospel to the nations, not pronouncing judgments on them. Judgment is postponed until the "day of wrath" (Rom. 2:5). Meanwhile, God waits patiently for the repentance of all men and women who will hear and believe the gospel. Also, the apostle Paul taught that the gift of prophecy was for building up the church—not the spiritual strong-arming of nations (Eph. 4:11–12).

Do Prophets Today Reveal New Truths?

Prophets today do not reveal new truths. By new truths, we mean teachings and practices that must be adopted by the global church. In other words, prophets today don't reveal teachings and practices that are equal to Scripture in authority because only Scripture has authority over the entire church.

Once the truths of the Christian faith were preserved in Scripture, Christians weren't to expect new truths from future prophets. Rather, they were supposed to safeguard the truths that had already been revealed once and for all. As Jude, Jesus' half-brother, wrote to a group of first-century Christians: "Beloved, although I was very eager to write to you about our common salvation, I found it necessary to write appealing to you to contend for the faith that was *once for all* delivered to the saints" (Jude 3; our emphasis). There is no biblical support for the idea that prophets today can reveal new truths.

Prophet-apostle Bill Hamon claims that Ephesians 3:4–5 supports his teaching that prophets continue to reveal new truths. But this passage does not teach that prophets in each generation would reveal new truths. It simply speaks about a specific new truth—the truth about Gentiles' inclusion in the church—that was revealed to prophets in the first-century. But even Hamon would say that contemporary prophets can't give revelation that is equal in inspiration or authority to Scripture. He says "only a false prophet" would ever do that.[4]

---

4   Bill Hamon, *Prophets and the Prophetic Movement*, xxiii.

In our assessment, Hamon doesn't meet his own standard. He says, on the one hand, that prophets can't give new revelation that is equal to Scripture. So far, so good. But on the other hand, he says that prophets *can* reveal "new truths," which he also refers to as "restored truths" and as "present truth." And—if we've understood him correctly—he teaches that all the "new truths" must be embraced by every Christian who wishes to take part in God's end-time plans for the church. By claiming that new truths must be embraced by all Christians, is he not claiming—in effect—that all Christians are bound by those truths? This claim can only be made for the teachings of Scripture.

The way NAR leaders receive their new teachings is through what they call "prophetic illumination"—that is, by receiving sudden, new understandings of passages of Scripture. Hamon says Martin Luther received prophetic illumination of Ephesians 2:8–9, which showed Luther that people are saved by faith in Christ alone.[5] But this is a false comparison and a misunderstanding of Luther.

Luther didn't claim to discover a new, hidden meaning of Ephesians 2:8–9. He simply claimed to understand more clearly what was already in Scripture. This leader of the Protestant Reformation—a movement based on the teaching of *sola scriptura* (Latin for "Scripture alone")—would recoil from the idea that he was a prophet revealing new truths.

The truths about salvation were never "lost." Certainly they were unknown to many who weren't able to study Scriptures for themselves. The invention of the printing press, a surge of literacy, and translations of the Bible in people's native languages went far in correcting this problem. What these people needed was to be able to read the Bible for themselves, not for prophets to give them new, hidden meanings of the Bible or extrabiblical revelation.

---

[5]   See chapter 5, where we discussed Hamon's teaching on this.

A New NAR Bible: The Passion Translation

A disturbing development has occurred in NAR: NAR followers now have their own translation of the Bible, the Passion Translation, produced by NAR apostle Brian Simmons of Stairway Ministries in Wichita, Kansas.

The translation is being released in installments; the first, *Song of Songs*, was released in 2011 (and updated in 2013). Other installments released to date include *The Psalms, Proverbs*, and *Letters from Heaven by the Apostle Paul* (including Galatians, Ephesians, Philippians, Colossians, and 1 and 2 Timothy).

Simmons claims the Lord visited him personally and commissioned him to make this new Bible.[a] He named it the Passion Translation since he saw a need for a translation that restores the Bible's potency "unfiltered and unveiled."[b] It's selling very well according to rankings on Amazon.com. Readers have responded enthusiastically, reporting that it has brought them to tears and caused them to grow in their "love relationship" with Jesus—and even that God "swept through the room" while they were reading it.

The popularity of this new translation is due, in no small part, to endorsements by influential apostles and prophets, including Ché Ahn, James Goll, and Bill Johnson.

This is troubling. This NAR Bible contains completely reworded verses, making it appear that the Bible supports NAR teachings. For example, Galatians 6:6, in the Passion Translation, speaks of a "transference of anointing" that occurs between "teachers" (read: apostles and prophets) and their followers. It says: "And those who are taught the Word will receive an impartation from their teacher; a transference of anointing takes place between them."[c] But look this verse up in any standard Bible translation, such as the New International Version or the English Standard Version, and you will see that it says nothing about a "transference of anointing." (We talk about NAR teaching on the transference of miracle-working power in chapter 12.)

So, what's going on here? How did Simmons arrive at his drastically different translation?

He claims he has composed it by working from the original languages of Hebrew, Aramaic, and Greek. The result, however, suggests that this so-called translation is not the product of careful scholarship at all. Perhaps he would say that prophetic illumination played a part. This certainly seems to be implied in endorsements. Ché Ahn states that Simmons has been "given revelation and insight into a deeper meaning of the Scriptures."[d] The idea that Christians need an apostle to give them "a deeper meaning" of the Scriptures is not sound.

What Christians need—and what they already have—are trustworthy translations of the Bible that are faithful to the earliest and most reliable manuscripts. A trustworthy translation of the Bible is produced by a large team of Bible scholars who have mastered the original biblical languages. That's how the major translations of the Bible have been made. But Simmons works as a lone translator. He claims to have five professional editors look at his work, but he has yet to reveal the identities of those individuals.[e] Simmons would have been wise to submit his work to a spectrum of biblical scholars with proven expertise in biblical languages and the translation of the Bible. One would hope that his process would be more transparent since he is translating the Word of God. He also admits that he does not claim to be a scholar of the original languages.[f] Though he uses the title "Dr." before his name, he did not receive his degree from a recognized academic institution, but rather from the Wagner Leadership Institute—an NAR organization that offers courses in subjects like dream interpretation and miracle-working.

In short, Christians don't need apostles like Brian Simmons to unfold "deeper," hidden meanings with new translations of Scripture. What they need is to read the Bibles we already have and apply its commands to their lives. Heaven forbid that this NAR Bible continues to grow in popularity. We pray that our generation of young people will be too discerning to believe the pretense that this is a trustworthy translation, or any kind of translation of the Bible. We pray that young men and women will use their spiritual gifts and natural abilities to be students of the sure Word, accurately handling the word of truth (2 Tim. 2:15).

a.   See Brian Simmons, "Song of Solomon, Part 1," YouTube video, 51:29, posted by HealingWaters, February 19, 2012; accessed June 18, 2014, https://www.youtube.com/watch?v=H8pmNZnlzlA.

b. Brian Simmons, *Letters from Heaven by the Apostle Paul*, The Passion Translation (Cicero, NY: 5 Fold Media, 2013), 9, Kindle edition. We note that in 2014 Simmons republished the Kindle edition of this book through another publisher, BroadStreet Publishing, LLC.

c. Ibid., 32. We note that Simmons has since substantially revised his translation of Galatian 6:6. It no longer speaks of a "transference of anointing" that takes place between teachers and their followers, but instead states that a "sharing of wealth takes place between them." This revised translation of Galatians 6:6 can be seen in the second edition of his book. See Brian Simmons, *Letters from Heaven by the Apostle Paul*, 2nd ed. The Passion Translation (Cicero, NY: 5 Fold Media, 2013), 31, paperback edition. In Simmons's earlier translation of Galatians 6:6, the reference to a "transference of anointing" correlates to a distinct doctrine within the NAR theological system. But Simmons modified his translation so that it does not parallel NAR teachings so closely. We wonder what basis Simmons had for shifting his translation in such a substantial way and doing so without explaining the need for a revision.

d. Brian Simmons, *Letters from Heaven by the Apostle Paul*, The Passion Translation (Cicero, NY: 5 Fold Media, 2013), 3, Kindle edition.

e. Any reader can go to the front matter of a standard translation of Scripture (King James Version, New American Standard Bible, New International Version, Revised Standard Version, English Standard Version, and the Holman Christian Standard Bible, for example) and see who served on the translation committees and learn what principles guided their translation work. We can only speculate that the reason Simmons has not revealed the identities of his editors is because they do not possess the scholarly credentials to qualify them for serving on a translation committee. If we are wrong, we welcome Simmons to correct us by revealing the identities of his editors.

f. Simmons made this statement on June 8, 2013, in a public discussion forum on Amazon.com (a statement he deleted on June 18, 2013). Documentation of Simmons' deleted comment is in the authors' possession. See Holly Pivec's "Customer Review" of *Letters from Heaven by the Apostle Paul*, "5 Reasons You Can't Trust *The Passion Translation*," Amazon.com, posted May 24, 2013; accessed June 29, 2014, http://www.amazon.com/review/R2M5CLW27ENVNE/ref=cm_cd_pg_next?ie=UTF8&asin=1936578565&cdForum=Fx89ILOZ20G44E&cdPage=2&cdThread=Tx3L111JG161C1U&store=books#wasThisHelpful.

TESTING NAR PROPHETS

NAR leaders warn that rejecting God's prophets leads to loss of re-ward and even to judgment, based on verses such as Matthew 10:41 and Psalm 105:15. Their misuse of these verses has made many of their followers afraid ever to question the teachings of NAR prophets. However, people should never be afraid to question the teachings of any church leader. Scripture commands Christians to test all prophe-cies (1 Thess. 5:20–21). And there are numerous warnings about the threat of false prophets. The New Testament also warns that loss of reward and judgment can come from accepting false prophets and false teachers (2 John 1:8–10).

The Bible gives three key tests for determining whether a proph-et is genuine or not. Curiously, these tests seem to be neglected by NAR leaders.

The Fulfillment Test

One test set forth in Scripture is the fulfillment test, which requires that prophets' predictions must come true. This test is given in Deu-teronomy 18:21–22, right after Moses predicts the rise of a series of prophets to come following his death. In other words, as soon as the Israelites learned that God would send them a series of prophets, God provided a clear test for distinguishing the prophets of God from the imposters.

> *And if you say in your heart, "How may we know the word that the LORD has not spoken?"—when a prophet speaks in the name of the LORD, if the word does not come to pass or come true, that is a word that the LORD has not spoken; the prophet has spoken it presumptuously. You need not be afraid of him. (Deut. 18:21–22).*

Though NAR leaders acknowledge that Old Testament proph-ets had to be one hundred percent accurate in what they predicted, many of them also claim that the same fulfillment test doesn't apply to NAR prophets. They claim this is because prophets in the New Testament are extended more grace.[6]

This teaching that genuine prophets can make mistakes when they prophesy is common in NAR. In support of this teaching, NAR leaders sometimes point to respected theologian Wayne Grudem, who agrees that New Testament prophets are not expected to be one hundred percent accurate in their prophecies.[7] But this is a shockingly bad misunderstanding of Grudem. Grudem states that New Testament prophets need not be one hundred percent accurate because they do not have the same level of authority as the Old Testament prophets and do not hold a formal governing office of the church.[8] Unlike Grudem, NAR leaders teach that New Testament prophets do have the same level of authority as Old Testament prophets and that they do hold a formal governing office. Thus, they misuse Grudem's teaching to support their view that NAR prophets can err and still be true prophets.

The fulfillment test applies to both Old and New Testament prophets since there is no indication that it was ever abolished. Christians today, of course, do not customarily stone false prophets, as required in the Old Testament (Deut. 13:5, 6–10; 18:20). This is partly because the church is not a nation under God's direct rule and is not under the Mosaic law. Nevertheless, the fulfillment test remains valid.

The offense of giving false prophecies is serious. When prophets falsely claims to speak for God, they are guilty of breaking God's third commandment: "You shall not take the name of the Lord your God

---

[6] Bill Hamon, *Prophets, Pitfalls and Principles: God's Prophetic People Today* (Shippensburg, PA: Destiny Image Publishers, 2001), 101; Mike Bickle, *Growing in the Prophetic: A Practical, Biblical Guide to Dreams, Visions, and Spiritual Gifts*, rev. ed. (Lake Mary, FL: Charisma House, 2008), 41, PDF e-book available at Mike Bickle.org; accessed August 14, 2014, http://mikebickle.org/books.

[7] Wayne Grudem, *The Gift of Prophecy in the New Testament and Today*, rev. ed. (Wheaton, IL: Crossway Books, 2000), 51–94.

[8] Ibid., 27, 160.

in vain, for the Lord will not hold him guiltless who takes his name in vain" (Exod. 20:7).

When many people think of taking God's name in vain, they think only of using his name disrespectfully. But taking God's name in vain also means to use it to deceive someone, as occurs when someone gives a false prophecy.

God, speaking through the prophet Jeremiah, condemned prophets who falsely claimed to speak for him.

> *I did not send the prophets,*
> *yet they ran;*
> *I did not speak to them,*
> *yet they prophesied. . . .*

> *Behold, I am against the prophets, declares the LORD, who use their tongues and declare, "declares the LORD." Behold, I am against those who prophesy lying dreams, declares the LORD, and who tell them and lead my people astray by their lies and their recklessness, when I did not send them or charge them. So they do not profit this people at all, declares the LORD.* (Jer. 23:21, 31–32).

In our view, it is an injustice that NAR prophets can give erroneous prophecies without suffering great harm to their reputations or any personal loss. But, unlike them, their followers aren't always left unscathed.

Of course, some mistaken predictions—such as those that implied that Mitt Romney would win the 2012 US presidential election—may not have devastating consequences.[9] But that is not always the case. Following mistaken predictions about the destruction of

---

[9] Bob Jones, "Hold On to Your Dreams," The Prophetic Ministry of Bob and Bonnie Jones, September 7, 2012; accessed February 22, 2014, http://www. bobjones.org/Docs/Words%20of%202012/2012_HoldOnToYourDreams. htm; Rick Joyner, "Lessons Learned from the Recent Elections—The Path of Life, Part 44," MorningStar Ministries, Week 51, 2012; accessed February 4, 2014, http://www.morningstarministries.org/resources/word-week/2012/ lessons-learned-recent-elections-path-life-part-44#.UvGRFbSmR8o.

Southern California made by prophet Rick Joyner and a colleague—predictions that the region would be attacked by terrorists and suffer a major earthquake—fear swept through charismatic churches.[10] Joyner's followers reportedly urged people to leave the state. These are the types of consequences that can occur when someone claims to speak with the authority of an Old Testament prophet, but is not held to the same level of responsibility.

The Orthodoxy Test

Another test Scripture gives for prophets is the orthodoxy test, which requires that prophets' words must line up with the revelation already given by God. This test is spelled out in Deuteronomy 13:1–5.

> If a prophet or a dreamer of dreams arises among you and gives you a sign or a wonder, and the sign or wonder that he tells you comes to pass, and if he says, "Let us go after other gods," which you have not known, "and let us serve them," you shall not listen to the words of that prophet or that dreamer of dreams. For the LORD your God is testing you, to know whether you love the LORD your God with all your heart and with all your soul. . . . But that prophet or that dreamer of dreams shall be put to death, because he has taught rebellion against the LORD your God, who brought you out of the land of Egypt and redeemed you out of the house of slavery, to make you leave the way in which the LORD your God commanded you to walk. So you shall purge the evil from your midst.

The orthodoxy test shows up again in the New Testament, where we see that all teachings in the churches—including teachings given by prophets—were held to the standard of teaching that had been handed down by the apostles of Christ. Consider, for example, the teaching that circulated in the church at Thessalonica—that the day of the Lord had already arrived. This teaching had come "by a spirit," possibly through the revelation of a false prophet (2 Thess. 2:2). The

---

[10]   Cedric Harmon, "God's Lightning Rod," *Charisma*, March 31, 2001; accessed March 1, 2014, http://www.charismamag.com/life/156-j15/features/issues-in-the-church/303-gods-lightning-rod.

apostle Paul countered it by reminding the Thessalonians what he had already taught them, that the day of the Lord wouldn't occur until other events took place first (2 Thess. 2:3–5).

Elsewhere, Paul urged his pupil Timothy to take the teachings he had learned from Paul—the apostolic teachings—and "entrust [them] to faithful men who will be able to teach others also" (2 Tim. 2:2). Notice that Paul didn't tell Timothy to look for new truths from prophets. He instructed him to recall truths already revealed through the apostles of Christ.

NAR leaders profess agreement with the orthodoxy test. They claim prophets' teachings must line up with Scripture. Our assessment is that many of their teachings do not line up.

Furthermore, many NAR leaders continue to esteem prophets who have promoted strange and even heretical teachings, including William Branham (1909–1965). The prophet Branham taught that Eve had sexual relations with the serpent (the so-called "serpent's seed" doctrine) and that those who are descended from the serpent seed are destined for hell—a non-eternal hell—while those who accept Branham's teachings are predestined to become the "bride of Christ." Branham also denied the doctrine of the Trinity.[11] These particular teachings of Branham are overlooked since he was known to have an unparalleled ministry of miracles. It is unwise to discount Branham's teachings while extolling his amazing miracles. Jesus warned about false prophets who will arise and perform miraculous signs and wonders (Matt. 24:24).

If an individual can promote such strange and heretical teachings and still be considered a true prophet within NAR, it seems that the orthodoxy test is not being applied consistently.

---

[11]   D. J. Wilson, "William Marion Branham," in *The New International Dictionary of Pentecostal and Charismatic Movements,* ed. Stanley M. Burgess (Grand Rapids: Zondervan, 2002), 440–41.

The Lifestyle Test

A third test Scripture gives for prophets is the lifestyle test. Jesus said false prophets could be known by their bad fruit—that is, by their lawless conduct.

> *You will recognize them by their fruits. Are grapes gathered from thorn-bushes, or figs from thistles? So, every healthy tree bears good fruit, but the diseased tree bears bad fruit. A healthy tree cannot bear bad fruit, nor can a diseased tree bear good fruit. Every tree that does not bear good fruit is cut down and thrown into the fire. Thus you will recognize them by their fruits.*
>
> *Not everyone who says to me, "Lord, Lord," will enter the kingdom of heaven, but the one who does the will of my Father who is in heaven. On that day many will say to me, "Lord, Lord, did we not prophesy in your name, and cast out demons in your name, and do many mighty works in your name?" And then will I declare to them, "I never knew you; depart from me, you workers of lawlessness."* (Matt. 7:16–23)

What would such lawless conduct include? Sexual immorality and idolatry are specifically associated with the false prophetess Jezebel at the church in Thyatira. Paul describes the false prophet Bar-Jesus as being a "son of the devil," an "enemy of all righteousness," and "full of all deceit and villainy" (Acts 13:10). Old Testament false prophets were characterized by greed (Mic. 3:5, 11; 2 Peter 2:15) and drunkenness (Isa. 28:7–8).

The lifestyle test is the most reliable test for prophets, according to Hamon.[12] He believes that, when evaluating a prophet, it's more important to look at the "quality of his life"—including his marriage, manners, and morality—than the accuracy of his prophecies. Hamon acknowledges that no prophet is perfect. But Christians should take note when any major area of a prophet's life is "seriously out of order."[13]

---

[12] Bill Hamon, *Prophets, Pitfalls and Principles*, 101.

[13] Bill Hamon, *Prophets and Personal Prophecy: God's Prophetic Voice Today* (Shippensburg, PA: Destiny Image Publishers, 2001), 125.

Hamon is right that lifestyle is a test for prophets. But this test alone is not enough. Outwardly, false prophets can sometimes look very good, disguising themselves, as Jesus said, "in sheep's clothing, but inwardly are ravenous wolves" (Matt 7:15).

Several NAR prophets whose significant moral failures have been publicly documented continue to be regarded as genuine prophets by many of their peers. Bob Jones—whose prophetic words were pivotal in guiding the ministries of many NAR leaders, including IHOP[14]— confessed in 1991 to sexual misconduct and the abuse of his prophetic office. This misconduct reportedly "consisted of encouraging women to undress in his office so they could stand 'naked before the Lord' in order to receive a [prophetic] 'word.'"[15] Despite such a gross abuse of his office, Jones remained influential as a prophet in NAR until his death in 2014. He was so revered that his memorial

---

[14] Mike Bickle, "A Worldwide Youth Movement: Prophetic and Intercession," IHOP's Prophetic History (Celebration Feast on Sept. 17–19, 2006); accessed August 30, 2014, http://www.mikebickle.org.edgesuite.net/MikeBickleVOD/2006/20060917_A_Worldwide_Youth_Movement_Prophetic_and_Intercession_Mike_Bickle.pdf, PDF file.

[15] See "Jones, Bob," Apologetics Index; accessed February 22, 2014, http://www.apologeticsindex.org/j00.html#jones. Bob Jones was removed from ministry in Vineyard churches in 1991 after confessing to sexual misconduct. See "Minister Removed After Confession of Sexual Misconduct," *The Olathe Daily News*, November 13, 1991; accessed February 4, 2014, http://www.religionnewsblog.com/16929/minister-removed-after-confession-of-sexual-misconduct. A letter written by Vineyard founder John Wimber and sent to Vineyard pastors, dated November 7, 1991 (a copy of which is in the authors' possession), states that Jones confessed to committing "serious sin," including "using his [prophetic] gifts to manipulate people for his personal desires" and "sexual misconduct." And a transcript of a taped message given by Mike Bickle following Jones's confession states that Jones "used his ministry gift and position to win the confidence of two women and then he did things to them," which included "disrobing" and "fondling." Mike Bickle, "Bob Jones' Discipline," undated transcript of a recording on audiocassette (November 1991?), in the authors' possession.

service was attended by prominent NAR leaders and was broadcast live, worldwide, by GOD TV.

Paul Cain—who confessed in 2005 to being an alcoholic and a long-term, practicing homosexual[16]—resumed public ministry in 2007. To the credit of some prominent NAR leaders—Mike Bickle, Jack Deere, and Rick Joyner—the validity of the restoration process was questioned.[17] Cain has since gone on to share a speaking platform with other NAR leaders, including Bill Hamon.[18] This raises the question: What type of behavior, in Hamon's mind, actually characterizes a life that is "seriously out of order"? And what are the consequences when an alleged prophet fails this test?

The lifestyle standard can be highly subjective. Hamon seems to have set aside the more objective fulfillment test. Scripture places an emphasis on the combination of these tests.

If NAR leaders are going to claim that prophets in NAR are genuine, they cannot simply ignore these biblical tests. These tests must be applied consistently and with due diligence since Scripture clearly teaches that false prophets pose a serious threat to the church.

---

[16] In October 2004, Paul Cain was publicly accused by his colleagues Rick Joyner, Jack Deere, and Mike Bickle of practicing homosexuality over a long period of time and being an alcoholic—allegations he first denied, but later confessed. See J. Lee Grady, "Prophetic Minister Paul Cain Issues Public Apology for Immoral Lifestyle," *Charisma*, February 28, 2005; accessed February 4, 2014, http://www.charismamag.com/site-archives/154-peopleevents/people-and-events/1514-prophetic-minister-paul-cain-issues-public-apology-for-immoral-lifestyle-.

[17] Mike Bickle, Jack Deere, and Rick Joyner, "Update on Paul Cain, Part 5," MorningStar Ministries, 2007; accessed February 19, 2014, 1http://www.morningstarministries.org/resources/special-bulletins/2007/update-paul-cain-part-5#.UwRurYV6V8o.

[18] Hamon and Cain were featured speakers at a 2011 conference titled *Global Call School of the Prophets*, held April 13–16, in Corona, California.

★★★

In summary, the Bible does not support the NAR teaching that prophets today must govern the church. Nor does it support the teachings that prophets today direct individuals in major life decisions, prophesy to nations, or reveal new truths. The Bible identifies three key tests for determining whether a prophet is genuine or not. But the consistent application of these tests by many NAR leaders is sketchy at best.

Now we turn to NAR teachings on spiritual warfare.

8

Strategic-Level Spiritual Warfare

In the countryside of England, about a dozen people, followers of contemporary apostles and prophets, drive the main roads coming into their small town. They exit their cars carrying three-foot wooden stakes that have been inscribed on the sides with verses of Scripture. They stop at each road, say a prayer, and then drive a stake into the ground. They believe their actions will prevent demons from influencing their town.

★★★

In Southern California, a small team of people are climbing to the top of the Hollywood Hills, overlooking the famous Hollywood sign. Led by an influential apostle, they recite the words of a "divorce decree" between the region and a powerful demon they call Baal. They pray to "uproot the perversion" of Hollywood's entertainment industry. Following their prayer, they feel a swift breeze in their midst and believe it is a signal that God heard their prayer and is "cleansing away the perversion."[1]

★★★

In Nepal, a team that has taken special training in Alpine climbing is scaling Mount Everest, the world's highest mountain. The team has named their expedition Operation Ice Castle. Their mission is to find the throne of a high-ranking demon they call the Queen of Heaven. They believe this demon rules over the 10/40 Window—the

---

[1] "California Root 52 Report," Generals International; accessed May 6, 2014, http://www.generals.org/prayer/root-52/prayer-reports/california-report/.

region of the world situated between the latitudes of 10 degrees and 40 degrees north, encompassing North Africa, the Middle East, and sections of Asia to Japan. At 20,000 feet, the team attempts to directly assault the evil spirit by building an ice altar where they engage in "warfare prayer," commanding the demon to leave. They also use an ice ax to write the words "Jesus lives" on the mountain.[2]

★★★

Though the actions of these people might seem strange to many, teams like these are active in small towns and large cities throughout the world. The followers of NAR apostles and prophets often go to prominent locations in their communities—such as their capitol building or the highest mountain—and engage in what they call prophetic acts to release God's power. These acts include driving stakes into the ground inscribed with passages of Scripture, taking Communion then burying the bread and wine, pouring kosher salt around the perimeters of the property, and anointing the site with oil. One team actually filled a balloon with anointing oil and bombed their target from an airplane.[3]

Though the specific acts they perform are different, and the locations to which they go vary, these teams share something in common. They are all attempting to wage spiritual warfare against powerful demons that rule over cities and nations. They believe casting out these demons from specific geographical regions is the best thing they can do to advance God's kingdom on earth.

This leads to an important question: How exactly can Christians advance God's kingdom on earth?

---

[2]   C. Peter Wagner, *Wrestling with Alligators, Prophets and Theologians: Lessons from a Lifetime in the Church—A Memoir* (Ventura, CA: Regal Books, 2010), 238–39. Other details of this operation are recorded by observers in Richard Salisbury and Elizabeth Hawley, *The Himalaya by the Numbers: A Statistical Analysis of Mountaineering in the Nepal Himalaya* (Seattle, WA: Mountaineers Books, 2012).

[3]   Kevin Reeves, *The Other Side of the River* (Eureka, MT: Lighthouse Trails Publishing, 2007), chapter 3.

Most traditional Christians believe the best way to advance God's kingdom is through sharing the gospel and sending out missionaries. But NAR apostles and prophets claim the church must also yield to the authority of modern-day apostles and prophets to whom God has given new strategies to advance his kingdom—a view known as dominionism.

Many of the dominionist strategies that have been received by today's apostles and prophets are related to an overarching strategy known as strategic-level spiritual warfare. In this chapter we explain NAR teachings on strategic-level spiritual warfare. In the next chapter we will evaluate these teachings in light of Scripture.

What Is Strategic-Level Spiritual Warfare?

Strategic-level spiritual warfare is the act of confronting powerful evil spirits that are believed to rule specific regions of the world. These spirits are called territorial spirits because they control different territories, like cities and nations.

Strategic-level spiritual warfare is based on the belief that the people living in these regions are kept in bondage by territorial spirits. As long as the territorial spirits are in control, no major advances can be made in sharing the gospel. So, first the spirits must be cast out. Then entire nations of people will respond to the gospel. This will bring about the fulfillment of a popular NAR prophecy known as the Great End-Time Harvest—the greatest harvest of souls in history, when more than a billion people will convert to belief in Christ. A common word image used by NAR leaders to describe strategic-level warfare is that of an air war on high-ranking demons that is necessary to pave the way for the ground troops of evangelists and missionaries.

Teachings about strategic-level spiritual warfare differ from traditional Christian teachings about spiritual warfare, which usually focus on resisting temptation, knowledge of Scripture, and, occasionally, casting out demons from individuals.

But territorial spirits cannot be ignored, according to NAR leaders. And they can't be cast out by just any Christian. Only an apostle has that authority. Apostle Héctor Torres calls the apostle "an arch rival to the forces in the heavenlies."[4] He writes: "Although every believer has rank to cast out devils [from individuals], apostles walk and minister in the highest rank. Evil spirits and angels recognize this rank."[5]

So NAR leaders teach that apostles must take the lead when engaging in this type of spiritual warfare.

KEY BIBLE PASSAGES USED TO DEFEND
NAR TEACHING ON STRATEGIC-LEVEL SPIRITUAL WARFARE

Daniel 10

One passage of Scripture commonly used by NAR leaders to defend strategic-level spiritual warfare is Daniel 10. This passage reveals that the archangel Michael was engaged in a battle against two specific evil spirits that ruled over kingdoms—"the prince of Persia" and the "prince of Greece" (Dan. 10:13, 20). According to a NAR understanding of this passage, the reason Michael was sent to battle these two evil territorial spirits was that the prophet Daniel had engaged in strategic-level spiritual warfare against them.

Ephesians 3:10

Peter Wagner, who has developed much of what is taught about strategic-level spiritual warfare, finds support for the direct confrontation of high-ranking demons in Ephesians 3:10, which states: "so that through the church the manifold wisdom of God might now be made known to the rulers and authorities in the heavenly places."

---

[4] Héctor Torres, *The Restoration of the Apostles and Prophets: How It Will Revolutionize Ministry in the 21st Century* (Nashville, TN: Thomas Nelson, 2001), 143.

[5] Ibid.

FRANK PERETTI NOVELS

In 1986, author Frank Peretti captured the imaginations of a generation of Christians with his bestselling novel *This Present Darkness* (Wheaton, IL: Crossway, 1986, 2003). This fictional book depicts, in vivid detail, a battle between small-town Christians and the demons ruling over their town, a place called Ashton. Though we do not know whether Peretti is affiliated with NAR, his book popularized NAR practices of strategic-level spiritual warfare.

Here is an excerpt from the book, in which Christians try to cast out the most powerful demon ruling over Ashton. The scene starts with a group of Christians trying to cast out a less-powerful demon named Witchcraft, who has inhabited a man named Bobby. The demon responds by calling for help from the more powerful demon.

The demon continued to cry out through Bobby, "Rafar . . . Rafar . . ."

"Who is Rafar?" Hank asked.

"Rafar . . . is Rafar . . . is Rafar . . . is Rafar . . ." Bobby's body twitched, and he spoke like a sickening broken record.

"And who is Rafar?" Andy asked.

"Rafar rules. He rules. Rafar is Rafar. Rafar is lord."

"Jesus is Lord," John reminded the demon.

"Satan is lord!" the demon argued.

"You said Rafar was lord," Hank said.

"Satan is lord of Rafar."

"What is Rafar lord of?"

"Rafar is lord of Ashton. Rafar rules Ashton."

Andy tried a hunch. "Is he prince over Ashton?"

"Rafar is prince. Prince of Ashton."

"Well, we rebuke him, too!" said Ron.

Of this verse Wagner writes: "Certain antiwar advocates would have us believe that, while we may command demons to leave individuals, we must not address higher-ranking spiritual beings. However, this Scripture specifically tells us that the Church—those of us who are believers—is expected to declare God's wisdom to principalities and powers."[6]

KEY PRACTICES RELATED TO
STRATEGIC-LEVEL SPIRITUAL WARFARE

How, in practical terms, can apostles cast out territorial spirits? We will now look at some of the key NAR practices associated with strategic-level spiritual warfare.

Spiritual Mapping

A foundational step in casting out a territorial spirit is a practice known as spiritual mapping. This involves researching a specific city or nation to discover the ways territorial spirits hinder the spread of the gospel in that particular geographical region. For example, John Dawson of Youth With a Mission believes that a "spirit of greed" was "let loose during the California Gold Rush and still dominates the culture of Los Angeles and San Francisco to this day."[7]

In many cases, spiritual mapping projects seek to determine not just what a territorial spirit does—such as promoting greed—but also the exact name of a territorial spirit. This is because many NAR leaders, like Wagner, believe that knowing the name of a demon gives Christians more power over that demon.[8]

To help identify the territorial spirits ruling over a specific city, spiritual mapping projects seek answers to questions about the city's

---

[6]   C. Peter Wagner, *Changing Church* (Ventura, CA: Regal Books, 2004), 117.

[7]   John Dawson, *Taking Our Cities for God* (Lake Mary, FL: Charisma House, 1989), 53–54.

[8]   C. Peter Wagner, *What the Bible Says About Spiritual Warfare* (Ventura, CA: Regal Books, 2001), 63–64.

history: Why was the city originally settled? What were the religious practices of the early inhabitants? What religious institutions have dominated in the city?

Spiritual mapping also involves surveying the present city. This includes identifying sites of occult activity (such as New Age bookstores), idolatry (such as buildings used for worship by non-Christian religions), or immorality (such as strip clubs). If many sites of a particular kind are discovered—for example, sites associated with witchcraft—then it might be decided that a territorial spirit associated with witchcraft controls a city.

When a territorial spirit is identified by name, it is often confronted. The confrontation may take place at a site believed to be the physical seat of the spirit's rule. Often this is the site of some non-Christian place of worship, such as a pagan temple, Masonic Lodge, or an Islamic mosque. Or it may be the highest mountain in the region.

Spiritual mapping was introduced to many Christians on a popular level in 1989 by Youth With a Mission's Dawson, through his bestselling book *Taking Our Cities for God*. So it should come as no surprise that spiritual mapping has been practiced by the organization's missionary teams.

And spiritual mapping, at least in its earlier years, was a major activity of the World Prayer Center in Colorado Springs, Colorado, an organization co-founded by Wagner and Ted Haggard in 1998 on the campus of New Life Church. A unit of the center, called the Observatory, was specially devoted to this practice.[9]

One of the most extensive spiritual mapping efforts was undertaken by the United States Reformation Prayer Network, led by prophet Cindy Jacobs. The network appointed coordinators to oversee spiritual mapping projects in each of the fifty US states. The information gleaned from the projects was compiled into prayer guides to be used by people taking part in a national prayer strategy called Root 52. For the entire year of 2010, participants in each state used the guides to

---

[9]   Wagner, *Wrestling with Alligators, Prophets and Theologians*, 241.

go to strategic locations and wage spiritual warfare against territorial spirits ruling in those states. This included performing prophetic acts.

Prayerwalking

Prayerwalking is the practice of sending teams to the physical locations of regions where they desire to see spiritual and societal transformation. These teams walk their neighborhoods, cities, or university campuses and engage in warfare prayer, which, according to Wagner, consists of issuing direct commands to territorial spirits to leave cities or to "stop some ungodly activity."[10] NAR leaders claim that prayerwalks can be found in the Bible, such as when the Israelites marched around the walls of Jericho (Josh. 6).

A prayerwalk may not be limited to one's local community. Long-distance prayerwalks, requiring travel to distant places, are often called prayer journeys and prayer expeditions. For example, on June 2, 2014, the Cindy Jacobs's United States Reformation Prayer Network announced plans to coordinate a continent-wide prayerwalk.[11] Called the USA Prayer Walking initiative, it would span the Americas, "from the tundra of Canada and Alaska to the tip of Argentina and Chile." The organization called for small teams of three to six Christians to volunteer to undertake portions of the prayerwalk between the dates of June 15, 2014, and July 31, 2014 by going to designated locations, including city hall buildings, college campuses, and sites of false worship.

Prayerwalking has also become a popular practice among more traditional churches that aren't aware of the NAR teachings that often lie behind the practice.

---

[10] Wagner, *What the Bible Says About Spiritual Warfare*, 38.

[11] "Stand for Right: An RPN Update," e-mail from United States Reformation Prayer Network to USRPN mailing list, June 2, 2014, http://us2.campaign-archive1.com/?u=2c8533b164a12dac690d3544f&id=0bb9d077bf&e=02548e3d54.

The Seven Mountain Mandate

So far we've looked at NAR practices for battling territorial spirits that rule specific regions of the world. But territorial spirits can also rule over societal institutions, according to many NAR leaders.

NAR apostles and prophets claim God has revealed a new strategy for advancing God's kingdom, a strategy they call the Seven Mountain Mandate. According to this revelation, the church must take control of the seven most influential societal institutions—called mountains—which are identified as government, media, family, business, education, church, and arts. These institutions are presently dominated by secular humanists and other people who do not share God's values. The church must take control of them if it is to fulfill its mandate to advance God's kingdom. The church's mandate to conquer these seven mountains is often compared to Israel's mandate to conquer seven nations before it could enter the Promised Land (Deut. 7:1).

In a book titled *The Seven Mountain Prophecy*, US prophet Johnny Enlow writes: "It's the Lord's plan to raise His people up to take every social, economic, and political structure of our nations."[12] Government is seen as one of the most important institutions because it makes laws that affect every other mountain. NAR leaders believe that God is in the process of raising up apostles to possess this critical mountain.

Another critical mountain is business, which controls wealth. When Christians possess this mountain, the wealth of the world will flow to the church so it can be used to advance God's kingdom. This will be the fulfillment of another popular NAR prophecy known as the Great End-Time Transfer of Wealth.

Though all NAR followers are taught to use their influence in their various places of work to transform society, special leaders called workplace apostles must rise to the highest positions within

---

[12]   Johnny Enlow, *The Seven Mountain Prophecy: Unveiling the Coming Elijah Revolution* (Lake Mary, FL: Creation House, 2008), 43–44.

the societal institutions. This is because only apostles have the God-given authority to cast out the territorial spirits that control those institutions. As Enlow writes, "Before we can fully displace powers and principalities, apostles will have to be properly positioned on the tops of the mountains. Again, an apostle is someone who has been given authority to displace top-of-the-mountain demons and bring the reign of heaven in their place."[13]

Enlow has identified the names of territorial spirits that presently control the institutions. Apollyon, for example, controls the media, Jezebel controls the arts. And because government is such a critical institution, it is controlled by none less than Lucifer.

Enlow has also identified the physical locations from which these territorial spirits rule. For example, he claims that New York City is the seat of Apollyon's rule. He suggests that NAR followers might go to New York City and engage in strategic-level spiritual warfare against this particular territorial spirit who controls the media.

★★★

In summary, NAR apostles and prophets claim that the best way for the church to advance God's earthly kingdom is by yielding to their authority and receiving the new strategies God has given them. Many of these strategies are related to an overarching strategy known as strategic-level spiritual warfare—the attempt to cast out powerful demons that rule over cities and nations.

---

[13]   Ibid., 66.

ORGANIZATIONS ENGAGED IN STRATEGIC-LEVEL SPIRITUAL WARFARE

Following are some influential US organizations that engage in strategic-level spiritual warfare.

Youth With a Mission (YWAM)

This charismatic, non-denominational missionary organization presently has more than 18,000 missionaries working in more than 180 countries. A number of YWAM missionary teams have engaged in practices of strategic-level spiritual warfare over the years, including spiritual mapping, prayerwalking, and identificational repentance.[a]

United States Reformation Prayer Network

This fifty-state network was founded by prophet Cindy Jacobs of Generals International. It seeks to mobilize 500,000 intercessors—10,000 in each US state—to reform the United States back to its biblical roots. The type of prayer promoted by Jacobs is referred to as "reformation intercession" and involves prayerwalking and other practices of strategic-level spiritual warfare.

Heartland Apostolic Prayer Network

This apostolic network—founded in 2006 under the apostle John Benefiel of Oklahoma City, Oklahoma—seeks to "change the heart of America and the Nations." Benefiel and other NAR leaders believe America has entered into an unholy marriage-type covenant with a powerful demon known as Baal. Thus, Heartland Apostolic Prayer Network encourages individuals and groups to take part in spiritual warfare ceremonies for "divorcing Baal." They believe the divorce will result in a spiritual revival and the end of societal evils, such as abortion. This network claims to have a leader and network in all fifty US states and to be represented in fifty nations.

Other Apostolic Prayer Networks in the United States

Apostolic prayer networks—which often engage in practices of strategic-level spiritual warfare—have formed in all fifty US states.

Many are affiliated with the United States Reformation Prayer Network and the Heartland Apostolic Prayer Network. These networks include:

- the Ohio Reformation Prayer Network,
- the Texas Apostolic Prayer Network,
- the Indiana Apostolic Prayer Network,
- the Louisiana Apostolic Prayer Network,
- the Illinois Apostolic Prayer Network,
- the Florida Apostolic Prayer Network,
- the Arkansas Apostolic Prayer Network,
- the Colorado Concert of Prayer,
- the Power Grid Apostolic Network (Kansas),
- the New England Apostolic Prayer Network,
- the Minnesota Apostolic Prayer Network,
- the Missouri Prayer Global Mission,
- Pray New York, and
- the Oklahoma Apostolic Prayer Network.

a. YWAM's involvement with strategic-level spiritual warfare is documented in René Holvast, "Spiritual Mapping: The Turbulent Career of a Contested American Missionary Paradigm, 1989–2005," PhD Dissertation, Utrecht University, 200), available as a PDF e-book at http://dspace.library.uu.nl/handle/1874/29340.

9

What the Bible Really Teaches About Spiritual Warfare

D oes the church need to cast out powerful ruling demons before the gospel can go forth and God's kingdom can advance? In this chapter we evaluate, in light of Scripture, spiritual warfare teachings and practices promoted by many NAR leaders.

IS STRATEGIC-LEVEL SPIRITUAL WARFARE BIBLICAL?

The Bible gives no support for the NAR teaching that powerful ruling demons, called territorial spirits, must be cast out before a city or nation can be reached with the gospel. There is not a single example in Scripture of God's people seeking to cast out a territorial spirit or engage such spirits in any way. Nor is there any teaching about the need for such engagement.

In Daniel 10, we do see evidence that territorial spirits exist—both fallen angels and good angels who have been assigned to rule over specific nations. The "prince of Persia" and the "prince of Greece"— evil spirits—are shown exerting control over the kingdoms of Persia and Greece. And the archangel Michael is shown ruling over Israel (Dan. 10:13; see also 12:1). But this passage gives no evidence that Daniel engaged in strategic-level spiritual warfare against the evil territorial spirits or that he was even aware of the battle raging between them and Michael until an angel revealed it to him (Dan. 10:1–20). He was merely engaged in fasting to show his identification with the suffering Jewish exiles.

As for the New Testament, Ephesians 3:10 does not state that Christians are to address territorial spirits, as Peter Wagner claims.

Rather, it states that God's wisdom is made known to angelic beings as they observe what God is doing through the church.

Though Christians have been authorized to cast out demons from individuals (Luke 10:17–19), the Bible gives no sign that they have been given the authority or responsibility to directly engage territorial spirits. Biblical scholar Clinton Arnold, who wrote a book addressing the practices of strategic-level spiritual warfare, writes: "It is therefore not necessary for us to discern them, name them, and try to cast them out. We are called to continue proclaiming the Word in the power of the Spirit and ministering the kingdom of God. We can have confidence that God will deal with these high-ranking spirits as He sees fit, just as He did for Daniel."[1]

Contrary to NAR teachings, Scripture indicates that rebuking such high-ranking spirits may actually be dangerous (Jude 8–10; 2 Peter 2:10–12). In Jude 9 we see that even the archangel Michael— one of the most powerful angels—did not dare to pronounce direct judgments on evil angels. Even Wagner acknowledges that taking on territorial spirits involves risk and "can result in casualties if not done wisely, according to spiritual protocol and under the specific direction and assignment of the Holy Spirit."[2]

So, at a minimum, attempts to cast out territorial spirits are futile. At worst, those who directly confront territorial spirits may be foolishly opening themselves up to powerful demonic attack.

Is Spiritual Mapping Biblical?

Since there is no biblical basis for directly confronting territorial spirits, then there also is no basis for spiritual mapping projects that seek to aid such confrontations through the identification of territorial spirits.

---

[1]   Clinton E. Arnold, *3 Crucial Questions about Spiritual Warfare*, 3 Crucial Questions (Grand Rapids: Baker, 1997), 185.

[2]   C. Peter Wagner, *Dominion! How Kingdom Action Can Change the World* (Grand Rapids: Chosen Books, 2008), 127.

One popular belief behind the practice of spiritual mapping is that knowing the name of a demon gives Christians more control over that demon. But Clinton Arnold points out that this belief, held by ancient occult practitioners, contradicts the teaching of Scripture. He writes:

> It seems to me that Paul wrote precisely against this kind of mind-set when he reaffirmed to the Ephesians that Christ had been raised "far above all rule and authority and power and dominion, *and every name that is named*" (Eph. 1:21 NASB [emphasis Arnold's]). Why do we need to find the name of a territorial ruler if we are in union with a Lord who has been exalted high above every conceivable power, regardless of its name or title?[3]

Not all spiritual mapping-type projects attempt to learn the names of territorial spirits or regions of their rule. Some simply create spiritual profiles of cities or nations to guide Christians on how to pray intelligently. These profiles may contain statistical information on the people living in a region, including information about their religious beliefs. An example is the popular prayer guide *Operation World*. These types of profiles, if they are viewed as evangelistic aids rather than as tools of strategic-level spiritual warfare, are helpful for the spread of the gospel.[4]

Prayerwalking

Prayerwalks, prayer journeys, and prayer expeditions have no biblical support, if they involve attempts to directly confront territorial spirits by saying warfare prayers. Prayer in the Bible is always directed to God; it is never directed to evil spirits.

But prayer *is* a weapon of spiritual warfare (Eph. 5:18–19). Arnold calls prayer "the heart and essence of spiritual warfare at any level."[5] It reflects our dependence on God to fight our battles for us. Thus,

---

[3] Arnold, *3 Crucial Questions about Spiritual Warfare*, 163.

[4] Ibid., 176–177.

[5] Ibid., 187.

even though it is inappropriate for believers to confront territorial spirits themselves, it is appropriate for them to pray to God and ask him to hinder any demonic spirits that oppose the spread of the gospel in a region.

The Israelites' march around Jericho cannot properly be used as an example of a NAR-type prayerwalk. The Israelites were not attempting to cast out a territorial spirit. They were demonstrating their faith in God to win a military victory for them. This was a one-time action, never again repeated in Scripture. It wasn't even the pattern for Israel's conquest of other cities in the land of Canaan at the time. Thus, it shouldn't be used to make prayerwalking a regular and vital practice.

That is not to say that all prayerwalks are unbiblical. They may be biblical if they're viewed simply as opportunities to pray in a more focused, fervent manner for the needs of a community. And, in a certain sense, these fervent prayers—to the degree that they reflect dependence on God—may be more effective than half-hearted prayers said from a remote location. But perhaps it's better not to think of such a practice as a prayerwalk at all because of the association with NAR teachings, but rather as petitionary prayer for our nations and cities.

The Seven Mountain Mandate

There is no biblical support for the teaching that territorial spirits must be cast out before the gospel can go forth and produce fruit in a city or nation. There is also no support for the idea that territorial spirits must be cast out of societal institutions, like the government, business, or media. Nor can the idea that apostles—specifically workplace apostles—have God-given authority to govern societal institutions be found in Scripture. New Testament apostles of Christ had a church office with authority to govern within the church. Their office and authority did not extend beyond the church into the sphere of the state or society.

It's praiseworthy for Christians to become experts in their fields and, through their influence, strive to make society as good as possible. But the Bible doesn't support the notion of workplace apostles who claim a far-reaching authority with power to govern outside of the church.

In their presentations of the Seven Mountain Mandate, NAR leaders often suggest that this strategy empowers all Christians—in whatever jobs or career fields they find themselves—to play significant roles in the transformation of society and the advancement of God's kingdom. This idea inspires many NAR followers. In truth, the Seven Mountain Mandate strategy is mostly empowering for NAR apostles, not for the average Christian. The truth is that many NAR leaders teach that only apostles have the authority to cast out demons ruling over the major societal institutions. The Seven Mountain Mandate strategy creates an elite class of workplace apostles. And it limits the most impactful ministry to those workplace apostles. If more NAR followers understood this, they might not embrace this NAR teaching with such enthusiasm.

★★★

In summary, the Bible does not support the NAR teaching that territorial spirits must be cast out of cities and nations before God's kingdom can be advanced—the teaching known as strategic-level spiritual warfare. Nor does it support the various NAR practices associated with this teaching, including spiritual mapping, prayerwalking, and the Seven Mountain Mandate.

In the next chapter we explain and evaluate with Scripture the NAR teaching known as apostolic unity.

10

Unifying the Forces Through Apostolic Unity

I n NAR, the church is an army that God is raising up to advance
his kingdom. But how can God's kingdom possibly advance
when Christians are divided into hundreds of denominations and
bicker endlessly about their differing beliefs? The secret for unifying
the church-army, according to many NAR leaders, is through Christians' submission to the leadership of apostles. This NAR teaching
is known as apostolic unity. In this chapter we examine this teaching and also evaluate it in light of the Bible's teachings about true
Christian unity.

APOSTOLIC UNITY

In NAR terms, apostolic unity occurs when the Christians in a giv-
en city unite under the leadership of apostles to transform their city.
An example can be seen in The Call assemblies held in large stadiums
throughout the United States. Co-founded by the apostle Ché Ahn
and the prophet Lou Engle, these assemblies bring together Christians from across denominations to fast and pray for the end of societal evils like abortion and homosexuality, and for the restoration
of the nation to its Christian roots. Apostolic unity is based on the
premise that apostles—not pastors—are the true spiritual gatekeepers
in a city. So for cities to see transformation, Christians living in those
cities must submit to the leadership of the local territorial apostles.

One such city that has experienced transformation under an apostle's leadership, according to NAR leaders, is Almolonga, Guatemala. Almolonga has become a popular NAR tourist attraction. It is
among four communities profiled in a documentary video produced

by George Otis Jr. called *Transformations*. According to the video, Almolonga—home to about 20,000 indigenous people—was once characterized by poverty, alcohol addiction, violence, ignorance, witchcraft, occult activity, and idol worship. Eventually, the vast majority of the population became born-again Christians, churches multiplied, and all the streets were named after biblical places.

A key to the transformation of Almolonga, according to the apostle Peter Wagner, was the leadership of territorial apostles whom God had assigned to govern in that specific city. One such apostle was Mariano Riscajche. Riscajche cast out from the city "numerous demons of alcoholism," planted a megachurch on the city's central plaza, and worked to help "establish a government of righteousness that succeeded in pushing Satan's government out of the territory."[1]

Prophet Chuck Pierce also teaches that apostolic leadership is the key to transforming cities. "If you want to see your city transformed, the Church in your region must understand God's use of apostles for this purpose. . . . We must recognize the divine government of the city that God is setting in place."[2]

NAR leaders attribute apostolic effectiveness to their access to vast resources. These resources come from the apostolic networks of churches and ministries they oversee. A network of churches and ministries—united in common cause under a common apostolic leader—is a powerful entity.

For all the power of individual apostolic networks, the apostle David Cannistraci believes there is a more powerful force on the horizon. When apostolic networks work with other apostolic networks the global church will finally achieve the unity needed to complete the Great Commission. Cannistraci writes: "Imagine what would happen if the leading apostles came together, heard from God and

---

[1] C. Peter Wagner, *Dominion! How Kingdom Action Can Change the World* (Grand Rapids: Chosen Books, 2008), 152.

[2] Chuck D. Pierce and Rebecca Wagner Sytsema, *The Future War of the Church: How We Can Defeat Lawlessness and Bring God's Order to the Earth* (Ventura, CA: Regal Books, 2001), 99–100.

committed the resources of their networks to reach a particular nation or people group! This kind of power could sweep the planet and reap the worldwide harvest almost overnight."[3]

But the church has not yet achieved unity because apostles have only just begun to be re-accepted. Speaking of an apostle's role in fostering church unity, Cannistraci cites George R. Hawtin, an early pioneer of NAR teachings, who wrote in 1951, "There shall never be any unity of faith until the ministry of the true apostle is recognized and obeyed as strictly in the last days as it was obeyed in the days of the apostle Paul."[4] Now that apostles are re-emerging, those in NAR believe, they can unify the church.

Apostolic unity, however, doesn't require unified doctrine. Many NAR leaders will work with others who may clash with their views, whether it be on Calvinism vs. Arminianism or the timing of the rapture. Oddly, many NAR apostles will partner with others who deny classically orthodox Christian doctrines. Wagner notes that some NAR leaders deny the doctrine of the Trinity,[5] such as those who are Oneness Pentecostals, for example.

Bill Johnson agrees that apostolic unity rather than doctrinal unity is the heart of Christian unity:

> While doctrine is vitally important it is not a strong enough foundation to bear the weight of His [God's] glory that is about to be revealed through true unity. . . . There are major changes in the "wind" right now. For the last several years people have started to gather around *fathers* instead of doctrine. . . . *Apostles are first and foremost fathers by nature . . . In the same way that a father and mother*

---

[3]   David Cannistraci, *Apostles and the Emerging Apostolic Movement: A Biblical Look at Apostleship and How God Is Using It to Bless His Church Today* (Ventura, CA: Renew Books, 1996), 196.

[4]   Ibid.

[5]   C. Peter Wagner, *Changing Church* (Ventura, CA: Regal Books, 2004), 157.

are to bring stability to a home, so the apostles and prophets are the stability of the Church [Johnson's emphasis].[6]

THE KEY BIBLE PASSAGE USED
TO DEFEND NAR TEACHING ON APOSTOLIC UNITY

What biblical evidence is used to support this NAR teaching? The key passage is Ephesians 4:11–13, where apostles are said to be given to the church to equip Christians "for the work of ministry, for building up the body of Christ, *until we all attain to the unity of the faith*" (our emphasis).

A major task of the apostles, then, is to help the church attain to the "unity of the faith."

APOSTOLIC UNITY COMPARED TO TRUE CHRISTIAN UNITY

NAR leaders rightly acknowledge the importance of Christian unity. This is emphasized in Jesus' High Priestly Prayer (John 17:20–23). The unity of Jesus' disciples would be a positive witness to the world (John 17:21, 23). Such unity characterized the fledgling church:

> *And all who believed were together and had all things in common. And they were selling their possessions and belongings and distributing the proceeds to all, as any had need. And day by day, attending the temple together and breaking bread in their homes, they received their food with glad and generous hearts, praising God and having favor with all the people. And the Lord added to their number day by day those who were being saved.* (Acts 2:44–47)

Church unity fostered the salvation of many people, as Jesus said it would.

This wasn't always the case. Serious divisions hindered the church at Corinth, as factions formed around various leaders (1 Cor. 1:11–12).

---

⁶ Bill Johnson, "Apostolic Teams—A Group of People Who Carry the Family Mission," The Elijah List, November 21, 2008; accessed April 24, 2012, http://www.elijahlist.com/words/display_word/7083.

The Corinthians disagreed sharply about church business (1:2–16), the Lord's Supper (11:17–34), and the exercise of spiritual gifts (12:1–14:40).

The apostle Paul admonished churches in Asia Minor to be "eager to maintain the unity of the Spirit in the bond of peace" (Eph. 4:3), showing humility, gentleness, patience, tolerance, and love (4:2). He didn't tell them to create unity; they were to maintain an already existing unity. What was the foundation of their unity? Their common faith. Paul says:

> *[being] eager to maintain the unity of the Spirit in the bond of peace. There is one body and one Spirit—just as you were called to the one hope that belongs to your call—one Lord, one faith, one baptism, one God and Father of all, who is over all and through all and in all.* (Eph. 4:3–6)

This is a problem for NAR teaching on apostolic unity. Their teaching requires submission to an apostle or group of apostles whom God has appointed to govern a specific city. It doesn't include shared commitment to core Christian beliefs. The unity Paul speaks of in Ephesians 4:11–13 is rooted in fundamental beliefs that include the doctrine of the Trinity. The context of this passage clarifies it further. Verses 14 and 15 stress knowledge and "speaking the truth":

> *And he gave the apostles, the prophets, the evangelists, the shepherds and teachers, to equip the saints for the work of ministry, for building up the body of Christ, until we all attain to the unity of the faith and of the knowledge of the Son of God, to mature manhood, to the measure of the stature of the fullness of Christ, so that we may no longer be children, tossed to and fro by the waves and carried about by every wind of doctrine, by human cunning, by craftiness in deceitful schemes. Rather, speaking the truth in love, we are to grow up in every way into him who is the head, into Christ.*

Apostolic unity in the NAR sense is not promoted in this or any other passage in the New Testament. In fact, rallying around certain church leaders was the source of division in the church at Corinth. Paul rebuked the Corinthians for tying their identities to various

Christian leaders: "For when one says, 'I follow Paul,' and another, 'I follow Apollos,' are you not being merely human?" (1 Cor. 3:4).

We believe Christians should lay aside relatively minor doctrinal differences and work together to advance God's kingdom. But essential Christian doctrines are nonnegotiable, even when so-called apostolic unity is at stake.[7]

Finally, we note one additional problem. Apostolic unity requires allowance of teachings that are completely absent from the Bible— teachings unique to NAR.[8] It is troubling to witness attempts at unity that minimize core Christian beliefs while demanding acceptance of doctrines with no Christian pedigree.

★★★

In summary, NAR leaders teach that, for God's kingdom to advance, Christians must unite under the leadership of today's apostles. But the New Testament teaches that the basis for Christian unity is shared commitment to core beliefs, not submission to apostles.

In the next chapter we explain NAR teachings about miracles.

---

[7] We note that in the article cited above, Bill Johnson does say, "there are doctrines that are essential to the Christian faith." He identifies one doctrine as an example: "Jesus is the eternal Son of God." We do not know whether he would identify the doctrine of the Trinity as non-negotiable. We also see no reason why he would compromise on this point. See Johnson, "Apostolic Teams."

[8] Recall our discussion of the Berean Principle in chapter 4.

11

A Miracle-Working Army

Mike felt that, to be a good Christian, he must manifest all the miracles that Jesus did—such as healing the sick and raising the dead. After all, Mike is a son of God, so he must do everything that Jesus, the Son of God, did while he was on earth. That's what Mike had been taught by the apostles and prophets he followed. He believed he was obligated to prove that Jesus was real by working great signs and wonders. He had even attended what was called a supernatural school of ministry at a local church so he could learn to work miracles.

But Mike felt like a failure when he wasn't able to work miracles. He would berate himself. "I could have healed this person," he thought, "if I had enough faith."

★★★

Vickie, a long-time charismatic, is the former director of a healing room in a small town in Canada. She first got involved with the healing room in hopes of seeing her own teen-aged daughter, Liz, healed of a congenital neuromuscular birth defect that confined her to a wheelchair. Vickie believed that God healed people in response to prayer and thought the healing room was a biblical ministry. But as time went on—and she attended training events hosted by the international organization with which the healing room was associated—she felt uncomfortable with a lot of the teachings she heard. They were taught by men who sincerely believed they were modern-day apostles whom God was raising up to lead the body of Christ—and in particular the thousands within the healing room ministry teams—to usher in the kingdom of God. She was dismayed that she never noticed these disturbing things prior to becoming director of a healing room.

★★★

Until recently, Marie attended a church influenced by contemporary apostles and prophets. She was startled to learn that her church was offering a class teaching people how to prophesy. "That seemed odd to me," Marie said. "I believe the ability to prophesy is a gift God gives to certain people. I don't think it's something you can learn to do."

★★★

Mike, Vickie, and Marie were taught that an important key for advancing God's kingdom is showing his miraculous power. People in NAR believe that miracles play a role in the church today. So do some more traditional Christians, especially Pentecostal and charismatic Christians. What sets their beliefs about miracles apart from the radical beliefs of people in NAR?

Many in NAR believe they will work miracles, like prophesying and healing the sick. They also believe they will be part of an army that will work greater miracles than the original apostles and prophets and even Jesus. This army is called by various names, including the Manifest Sons of God and Joel's Army. Some believe they'll continue to grow in miraculous power until they overcome sickness and death and call down God's fiery judgments on the wicked. And—most importantly—they believe they can learn to work miracles by following contemporary apostles and prophets.

In this chapter we explain NAR teachings about miracles. In the next chapter we evaluate them in light of Scripture.

LEARNING TO WORK MIRACLES

Rick Joyner has declared, "Parting the Red Sea will hardly be remembered as a significant miracle after the things that will be done by those who serve the Lord at the end of this age."[1] Joyner and other NAR leaders teach that the miracles to be worked by their followers will be greater than those that were performed by Jesus himself. Jesus multiplied bread and fish twice, but these apostles claim they will multiply food and other resources routinely. Jesus healed individuals, but they will heal all the people within a hospital simply by laying their hands on the building.

Two things set NAR apart from classical Pentecostals and charismatics: the magnitude of the miracles they work and the way they're empowered to do these things. Put simply: Many NAR people believe they can *learn* to work miracles. Pentecostals and charismatics do not.

To learn to work miracles, they read books like *When Heaven Invades Earth: A Practical Guide to a Life of Miracles*, by the apostle Bill Johnson. They attend conferences like the Supernatural Lifestyle Conferences sponsored by Kevin Dedmon Ministries. And many NAR churches offer classes that teach people how to heal people or prophesy. These books and classes present new truths that God has allegedly revealed to the apostles and prophets—teaching and practices that will activate (or release) the miraculous gifts of the Holy Spirit in individuals.

Those who are really serious about working miracles receive training in schools of supernatural ministry that have formed at churches. Many of these schools are associated with Bill Johnson's Bethel Church in Redding, California. Bethel Church's School of Supernatural Ministry—a full-time program—was founded in 1998 with only 36 students. It has since grown substantially, reporting more than 1,800 students during the 2012–2013 school year.[2]

Bethel students not only learn to work miracles themselves, but also how to teach other Christians to work miracles. Students take

[1]   Rick Joyner, *The Apostolic Ministry* (Wilkesboro, NC: MorningStar Publications, 2004), 42.

[2]   "Mission," Bethel School of Supernatural Ministry; accessed February 23, 2014, http://bssm.net/about/mission.

church members into their communities to participate in what are called Treasure Hunts.

Treasure Hunts are a form of supernatural evangelism, also known as prophetic evangelism. The hunts are conducted by teams of three or four people who rely on miraculous gifts of the Holy Spirit—including prophecy and healing—to share God's love with people. Before a Treasure Hunt, team members ask God to give them prophetic words of knowledge—also called clues—about specific people they'll find in the community. The clues they seek include a person's name, descriptions of the person's appearance, and any ailments that person may have (such as recurring headaches or a bad knee).[3] Students mark these clues on a treasure map, which they use to guide them to a person—called a treasure—who matches their clues.

Here's an example recounted by a team member. During one Treasure Hunt conducted in a Wal-Mart, the clues included "Starbucks coffee," "hurt right arm," and "frozen foods." The treasure hunters located a woman buying Starbucks coffee-flavored ice cream in the frozen food section. When they approached the woman and told her about their activity, she looked at their list of other clues and revealed that she had an injured right arm. She allowed the team members to pray for her and her arm was immediately healed.[4]

Adults aren't the only ones who must learn to work miracles. Children, too, are trained to work miracles. Some NAR churches do this by holding weekly PowerClubs, founded by the organization Kids in Ministry International. Unlike more traditional church clubs, such as Awana, where children study the Bible, PowerClubs teach children to work miracles, like prophesying and healing people.

---

[3] We obtained these details about the practice of Treasure Hunts from a book written by Kevin Dedmon, who teaches at the Bethel School of Supernatural Ministry and oversees the school's Treasure Hunt outreaches. See Kevin Dedmon, *The Ultimate Treasure Hunt: A Guide to Supernatural Evangelism through Supernatural Encounters* (Shippensburg, PA: Destiny Image Publishers, 2007), Kindle edition.

[4] Dedmon, *The Ultimate Treasure Hunt*, 23.

Many NAR churches train children to work miracles in their Sunday school classes. At Bethel Church, children are encouraged to talk with angels, interpret each other's dreams, and practice raising the dead by wrapping each other in toilet paper like mummies.[5] This also happens at churches that have no affiliation with NAR. One father grew concerned when he learned that the children's ministry director at his charismatically inclined, non-denominational church in Southern California adopted the teaching materials on miracles used at Bethel Church. The materials were phased out after he and others in the church voiced their concerns.

For some in NAR, the aim of these teachings is to overcome sickness and death.

But how will they do this?

Those who embrace new truths revealed by NAR apostles and prophets will begin to enjoy Divine Health. George Warnock (1917–2007), a pioneer of this teaching, says they can expect to live a thousand years.[6] And elderly followers will experience a reverse aging process, growing physically younger, says Joyner.[7] Joyner also says those who embrace this teaching will be able to heal every physical condition and that "there will be no plague, disease, or physical condition, including lost limbs, AIDS, poison gas, or radiation" that they won't be able to heal.[8]

---

[5] C. Hope Flinchbaugh, "Ignite the Fire," *Charisma*, February 28, 2007; accessed May 27, 2014, http://www.charismamag.com/site-archives/146-covers/cover-story/2172-ignite-the-fire. The Bethel Redding website features a video of the children's pastor Seth Dahl describing the supernatural activities in Bethel Church children's classes. See "Children's Ministry," Bethel Redding; accessed February 20, 2014, http://bethelredding.com/ministries/children.

[6] George H. Warnock, *The Feast of Tabernacles* (N.p.: The Church in Action, 1951; repr., 1980), chapter 12, Kindle edition.

[7] Joyner, *The Apostolic Ministry*, 171.

[8] Rick Joyner, *The Harvest* (Pineville, NC: MorningStar Publications, 1989), 167–68.

TYLER JOHNSON AND THE DEAD-RAISING TEAM

Tyler Johnson graduated from Biola University in Southern California. Later he veered from his conservative theological training. He enrolled at the Bethel School of Supernatural Ministry in Redding, California, where students are taught to work miracles. Tyler credits his 180-degree turn in theological outlook to a pivotal moment in his life. When his father had a sudden heart attack and died in Tyler's arms, Tyler became convinced that Christ's sacrifice on the cross meant that people no longer have to lose loved ones through death.[a] He started a Dead-Raising Team that goes to funeral homes and morgues at the request of grieving loved ones and prays for the dead to be raised. As of May 2014, the team claimed to have seen eleven resurrections, though no documentation has been provided.[b] They also go to churches to train others to raise the dead. Some thirty-eight other Dead-Raising Teams, they claim, have been established in twelve US states, Canada, and the Netherlands. Apostle Bill Johnson has publicly praised Tyler Johnson for starting the Dead-Raising Team.[c]

a. "The Dead Raising Team Founder," Dead Raising Team, N.d.; accessed June 13, 2014, http://www.deadraisingteam.com/DRT/Tyler_Johnson.html.

b. "Welcome to the Dead Raising Team," Dead Raising Team, N.d.; accessed May 29, 2014, http://www.deadraisingteam.com/DRT/Welcome.html.

c. Bill Johnson, audio, 3:18, from an undated message [given at Bethel Church in Redding, California?], from Dead Raising Team, accessed May 29, 2014, http://www.deadraisingteam.com/DRT/Info.html.

This doesn't stop at enjoying Divine Health. Followers will actually become immortal, according to Bill Hamon. That is, they will never die.

Before we explain Hamon's teaching on immortality, we note that Hamon often uses loose and ambiguous language in his writings, so that his teachings are not always clear. That said, Hamon apparently believes that Christians who follow end-time apostles and prophets will become immortal. When they accept the final new truth revealed by apostles and prophets, their mortal bodies will be instantly transformed into their eternal bodies.[9]

Hamon's teaching that Christians can become immortal through the reception of new truths is extreme, even for NAR. We emphasize that not all NAR leaders agree with this teaching. It's important, however, to address Hamon's teaching since he's one of the most influential contemporary prophets. His books that promote this teaching—including *Apostles, Prophets, and the Coming Moves of God*—are endorsed by influential NAR leaders, including Peter Wagner, Cindy Jacobs, and David Cannistraci. They're also sold by the Forerunner Bookstore at Mike Bickle's IHOP

The notion that the followers of end-times apostles and prophets could become immortal did not originate with Hamon. It was also taught by leaders in the post-World War II Latter Rain movement, including George Warnock. He taught that some would become immortal *before* Christ's return.[10]

Unlike Warnock, Hamon seems to believe that the transformation of believers' bodies will occur at Jesus' return, as other Christians also believe. However, most Christians believe that the transformation of their bodies will be accomplished by Christ—with no involvement of apostles, prophets, or new truths.

NAR followers receive their immortal bodies so they will have unlimited abilities to subdue the earth.[11] Hamon says, "The army of the Lord will progress on in the war until they have accomplished all they can in their limited mortal bodies."[12] Equipped with unlimited miraculous power, they will execute the judgments of God described in the book of Revelation.

---

[9]   Bill Hamon, *Apostles, Prophets, and the Coming Moves of God: God's End-Time Plans for His Church and Planet Earth* (Santa Rosa Beach, FL: Destiny Image Publishers, 1997), 263, 265.

[10]   Warnock, *The Feast of Tabernacles*, chapter 14.

[11]   Hamon, *Apostles, Prophets, and the Coming Moves of God*, 265.

[12]   Ibid.

This army of NAR revolutionaries may begin executing judgment before they receive their immortal bodies. Mike Bickle teaches that the end-time church will loose Jesus' judgments on the wicked. He seems to believe this will begin before Christ returns. The judgments to be loosed are the plagues described in the book of Revelation, including hail, falling stars, and an army riding fire-breathing horses; these will destroy one-third of the earth's population.[13] They will loose these judgments by saying what he calls "prayers of faith."

> I'm talking about the prayer of faith that heals, and I'm talking about the prayer of faith that kills. Yes, I said, "kills." . . . We're talking about heavenly arsenal from heaven striking people and resources. . . . I'm talking about cities, whole resources centers, will be destroyed.[14]

The idea that Christians will loose God's judgments comes from a totally new interpretation of the book of Revelation. Most Christians who believe that Revelation is about events that will occur in the end time believe that Christians alive at that time will be raptured to Christ before he releases his judgments on earth.[15] Those who believe the church will not be raptured first do not believe that they

---

[13] See Rev. 9:18. Some scholars believe this army is not an army of humans riding horses, but rather a demonic army. For Bickle's teaching on the church "loosing" the trumpet judgments, see Mike Bickle, "Session 1: Introduction and Overview of the Book of Revelation," *Studies in the Book of Revelation*, twelve-part series taught at the International House of Prayer University, Spring Semester 2014, available at MikeBickle.org; accessed May 6, 2014, http://www.mikebickle.org.edgesuite.net/MikeBickleVOD/2014/20140207_Introduction_and_Overview_of_the_Book_of_Revelation_BOR01_study%20notes.pdf.

[14] Mike Bickle, "IHOP TV Podcast 3," YouTube video, 10:59, posted by onething TV, December 3, 2008; accessed August 30, 2014, http://www.youtube.com/watch?v=K5FMsDrNyn4.

[15] The pre-wrath interpretation does not view the seals, but only the trumpets and bowls, as God's wrath; hence, in the pre-wrath view the church will experience the first six seals. See Alan Kurschner, *Antichrist Before the*

will have any part in loosing the judgments. In contrast to the majority of Christians, Bickle believes the church will remain on earth during the judgments, and that it will be actively involved in loosing those judgments.

All miracle-working power promised to NAR followers, enabling them as an army of God to loose divine judgments on earth and even overcome death for themselves, depends on accepting the new truths revealed by NAR apostles and prophets.

KEY BIBLE PASSAGES USED TO DEFEND NAR TEACHING ON MIRACLES

The following three passages of Scripture are used to defend NAR teachings about miracles. There are others, but these are especially prominent.

John 14:12

A favorite is John 14:12. This verse records a promise Jesus made to his disciples—a promise that those who believed in him would do "greater works" than he did while he was on earth. NAR leaders say this verse supports their teaching that the followers of apostles and prophets will work more amazing miracles than Jesus did: "Truly, truly, I say to you, whoever believes in me will also do the works that I do; and greater works than these will he do, because I am going to the Father."

2 Kings 6:1–2

NAR leaders claim that their schools of supernatural ministry, where they train people to work miracles, have support in the Old Testament. They say that Old Testament prophets, including the prophet Elisha, ran schools for the purpose of training young prophets. Elisha's

---

Day of the Lord: What Every Christian Needs to Know About the Return of Christ (Pompton Lakes, NJ: Eschatos Publishing, 2013).

school is mentioned in 2 Kings 6:1–2. NAR interpreters believe that the phrase "sons of the prophets" used in this passage refers to Elisha's students: "Now the sons of the prophets said to Elisha, 'See, the place where we dwell under your charge is too small for us. Let us go to the Jordan and each of us get there a log, and let us make a place for us to dwell there.' And he answered, 'Go.'"

Romans 8:19–23

Many NAR leaders cite Romans 8:19–23 to support their belief that the followers of apostles and prophets will have unprecedented miraculous powers that will be used to usher in God's kingdom. This NAR teaching is known as the Manifest Sons of God. Its name comes from language in the King James Version translation of this passage.

> *For the earnest expectation of the creature waiteth for the manifestation of the sons of God. For the creature was made subject to vanity, not willingly, but by reason of him who hath subjected the same in hope, because the creature itself also shall be delivered from the bondage of corruption into the glorious liberty of the children of God. For we know that the whole creation groaneth and travaileth in pain together until now. And not only they, but ourselves also, which have the firstfruits of the Spirit, even we ourselves groan within ourselves, waiting for the adoption, to wit, the redemption of our body.*

On the NAR interpretation, creation is waiting for the manifestation—or unveiling—of the sons of God so they can free it from the curse of decay and death. These sons of God—sometimes referred to as "little gods"—are the followers of end-time apostles and prophets who are patterned after the original Son of God, Jesus Christ. When they are manifested, these sons of God will develop superhuman powers. On some accounts (Hamon), they will even overcome death. The overcoming of death, proponents say, is referred to in verse 23, which speaks of the redemption of the believer's body. Together, these manifest sons of God will become a type of corporate Christ—a literal extension of the incarnation of Christ on earth.[16] This teaching about the arrival of a corporate Christ is often described as the church "giving birth" to the "many membered man-child."

Specific New Truths that Will Empower People to Work Miracles

People can learn to work miracles by adopting the new truths revealed by apostles and prophets. These are new truths about the following practices.

The Laying On of Hands

Miraculous gifts—such as gifts of physical healing or prophesying—can be transferred from apostles and prophets to others through a practice known as the laying on of hands.[17] This practice is promoted by countless NAR leaders.[18] Many NAR conferences feature a time for the transference of gifts, when attendees come forward and receive the laying on of hands by an apostle or prophet.

Fasting from Food

A breakthrough of unprecedented miraculous power in the church is planned by IHOP, which has instituted a Global Bridegroom Fast,

---

[16]   Hamon says the church is the "*full* expression of Christ Jesus, as Jesus is the full expression of His heavenly Father" [our emphasis]. He also says, "While Jesus was on Earth, His natural body was the home and headquarters of God here on Earth. Now the Church, as the corporate Body of Christ, is the home and headquarters for Jesus Christ here on Earth." See Bill Hamon, *The Day of the Saints: Equipping Believers for Their Revolutionary Role in Ministry* (Shippensburg, PA: Destiny Image Publishers, 2002), 73–74.

[17]   Hamon, *Apostles, Prophets, and the Coming Moves of God*, 192–93, 283.

[18]   See, for example, Bill Johnson, *When Heaven Invades Earth: A Practical Guide to a Life of Miracles* (Shippensburg, PA: Destiny Image Publishers, 2003), 79, Kindle edition.

held the first Monday through Wednesday of every month, and seven consecutive days beginning on the first Monday in December, until Christ returns.[19] IHOP founder Mike Bickle teaches that the rewards of fasting include miraculous power in personal ministry and the release of unprecedented prophetic revelation in the end time. This will include God's dispatching angels to some of his end-time prophets to bestow special understanding.[20]

24/7 Prayer

Non-stop, around-the-clock prayer, popularly known as 24/7 prayer, is another key to releasing miraculous power in the church. IHOP operates a Prayer Room, where continual prayer and worship have been held twenty-four hours a day, seven days a week, since 1999. And IHOP-style prayer rooms have opened in cities across the United States and around the world. More is going on here than the gathering of Christians to pray. These rooms prepare prayer warriors for their end-time role in loosing divine judgments against the Antichrist's kingdom.

Soaking

The purpose of this practice is to experience greater intimacy with God by soaking in his presence. It is believed that such intimacy will activate miraculous gifts and supernatural experiences. Soaking often involves elements such as finding a place of solitude, praying in one's native language and speaking in tongues, and then waiting to experience God's manifest presence. This presence may be mediated by dreams, visions, trances, out-of-body experiences, angelic visitations,

---

[19] "Global Bridegroom Fast," International House of Prayer; accessed December 3, 2013, http://www.ihopkc.org/about/global-bridegroom-fast.

[20] Mike Bickle and Dana Candler, *The Rewards of Fasting: Experiencing the Power and Affections of God* (Kansas City, MO: Forerunner Books, 2005), 24–27, PDF e-book, available at Mike Bickle.org; accessed August 14, 2014, http://mikebickle.org/books, PDF e-book.

or being transported in the Spirit, rather like Philip, an early Ethiopian convert who was miraculously transported between geographical regions (Acts 8:39–40).[21] People in NAR will also sometimes purchase soaking music to aid in their soaking experience.

Speaking in Tongues

Speaking in tongues—that is, speaking in a heavenly language—is seen as a key to activating other miraculous gifts.[22] At prophetic workshops led by Bill Hamon, where participants learn to prophesy, people are encouraged to engage in an activation exercise that involves finding a partner, starting to speak in tongues, and then saying out loud whatever comes into their mind as a prophetic word for their partner.

It's important to understand that some of the practices identified above (for example, fasting and speaking in tongues) are also practiced by Christians who are not part of NAR. But within NAR, these are often seen as *keys for learning to work miracles*. This is very different from the way Christians typically view these practices.

★★★

In summary, many people in NAR believe they'll be part of an end-time army that will work greater miracles than the original apostles and prophets and even Jesus. Some believe they'll continue to grow in miraculous power until they overcome sickness and death and call down God's fiery judgments on the wicked. They can learn to work all these miracles by following contemporary apostles and prophets, who reveal new truths for activating the miraculous gifts of the Holy Spirit in themselves.

---

[21]   Gary Oates, "Soaking: The Key to Intimacy with God," The Elijah List, January 9, 2012, accessed December 5, 2013, http://www.elijahlist.com/words/display_word.html?ID=10620.

[22]   Bill Hamon, *Seventy Reasons for Speaking in Tongues: Your Own Built In Spiritual Dynamo* (Shippensburg, PA: Destiny Image Publishers, 2012), 137.

12

What the Bible Really Teaches about Miracles

Now that we've explained NAR teachings on miracles, we evaluate these teachings in light of Scripture.

WILL THE MIRACLES PERFORMED BY THE FOLLOWERS OF NAR APOSTLES AND PROPHETS BE MORE AMAZING THAN THOSE PERFORMED BY JESUS?

Many NAR apostles and prophets claim that their followers will work more amazing miracles than the original apostles and prophets did—and even more amazing than those Jesus worked while he was on earth. They say this was the meaning of Jesus' promise to his disciples in John 14:12—that his followers would do "greater works" than he did: "Truly, truly, I say to you, whoever believes in me will also do the works that I do; and greater works than these will he do, because I am going to the Father." But that is not the meaning of Jesus' promise.

JOHN 14:12 AS TRANSLATED IN THE PASSION TRANSLATION (A NEW NAR BIBLE):

"I tell you this timeless truth: The person who follows Me in faith, believing in Me, will do the same mighty miracles that I do—even greater miracles than these because I go to be with My Father!"[a]

a.   Brian Simmons, trans., John: *Eternal Love, The Passion Translation* (Racine, WI: BroadStreet, 2014). See our evaluation of The Passion Translation in chapter 7.

So what is the meaning? As you might expect, scholars disagree. Some believe that Jesus promised that all his followers would work miracles. Others believe that Jesus may not have been referring to miracles at all, but to all the wonderful things they would do in the power of the Spirit, like sharing the gospel, teaching God's Word, and performing deeds of love and compassion.

For the sake of argument, let's allow that Jesus' promise was about miracles. If that's the case, the need for present-day apostles and prophets evaporates. Why? Because Jesus' promise has been available to *all* of his followers throughout history—to "whoever believes in him," as it says John 14:12. The promise is not just for a spiritual elite who follow end-time apostles and prophets.

Still, we must ask, in what way could the works of Jesus' followers be described as greater than his own? Does greater mean more amazing? No. On this point scholars agree. What could possibly be more spectacular than calming storms, giving sight to the blind, and raising the dead?

So what are the greater works Jesus spoke of? Some think the deeds of Jesus' followers would be greater because they influence more people. Jesus' disciples did spread out after his departure and were not confined to a single geographical region; and their work was remarkably fruitful, even revolutionary (see Acts 16:19–21; 17:6; 19:23–29).

But there's more to consider. "Greater" probably also refers to the enlargement of Jesus' works and a fuller understanding of them following the resurrection and through these men. D. A. Carson writes of this passage:

> Both Jesus' words and his deeds were somewhat veiled during the days of his flesh; even his closest followers . . . grasped only part of what he was saying. But Jesus is about to return to his Father, he is about to be glorified, and in the wake of his glorification his followers will know and make known all that Jesus is and does, and

their every deed and word will belong to the new eschatological age that will then have dawned.[1]

The full significance of all that Jesus taught and did during his earthly life would come into sharp focus following the resurrection. The incident on the road to Emmaus is a striking display of this (Luke 24:13–34). During one of Jesus' earliest post-resurrection appearances he explained more fully the truth about himself to men who should have recognized him and did not until he broke bread with them. They were galvanized to spread the word. Very soon after, Jesus showed up again, quite unexpectedly. The same thing happened: Jesus "opened their minds to understand the Scriptures" (Luke 24:45), and related it all to what he had told them "while I was still with you," it says (verse 44).

This would be *their* work, as well. For all that Jesus said and did during his earthly life, his resurrection was yet future. But his disciples would be eyewitnesses to the resurrected Lord. Their lives would be turned around. And their proclamation of the resurrection and its saving power would be spread throughout the world. From that point on, the world would never be the same.

Likewise, our work today has increased significance because what we profess about our faith can be seen in light of Jesus' finished work on the cross and by the power of his resurrection (see Rom. 1:16; 1 Cor. 1:18). Paul makes a stunning comparison between "signs" and "the power of God" in 1 Corinthians 1:22–24:

"For Jews demand signs and Greeks seek wisdom, but we preach Christ crucified, a stumbling block to Jews and folly to Gentiles, but to those who are called, both Jews and Greeks, Christ the power of God and the wisdom of God."

To appreciate this fully, you need to read also verses 26–31.

---

[1]   D. A. Carson, *The Gospel According to John*, The Pillar New Testament Commentary (Grand Rapids: Eerdmans, 1991), 496.

CAN PEOPLE LEARN TO WORK MIRACLES?

A key teaching of NAR is that people can learn to work miracles. NAR leaders claim that miraculous gifts can be activated in all those who accept the new truths that are taught by present-day apostles and prophets.

This concept of activating the gifts is foreign to the New Testament. The apostle Paul wrote that the miraculous gifts of the Holy Spirit are exactly that— *gifts*. They're not powers that can be learned. And they're distributed directly by the Holy Spirit to individuals as he alone decides (1 Cor. 12:11). They cannot be acquired by individuals at will.

Furthermore, Paul makes it very clear that not all can have each of these gifts. He asks rhetorically, "Are all apostles? Are all prophets? Are all teachers? Do all work miracles? Do all possess gifts of healing? Do all speak with tongues? Do all interpret?" (1 Cor. 12:29–30). The intended answer? No. Not all have the gift of prophesying, or the working of miracles, or healing. NAR teaching that miraculous gifts can be learned by any who desire them conflicts with Scripture in those places where gifts are addressed most fully.

> *To each is given the manifestation of the Spirit for the common good. For to one is given through the Spirit the utterance of wisdom, and to another the utterance of knowledge according to the same Spirit, to another faith by the same Spirit, to another gifts of healing by the one Spirit, to another the working of miracles, to another prophecy . . . (1 Cor. 12:7–10)*

What about the schools of the prophets found in the Old Testament? It's true that groups of prophets banded together and formed communities. But there is no sign that these companies of prophets were schools where people learned to prophesy. Rather, they were simply communities made up of people who already were prophets.

The idea that individuals can learn to heal or prophesy by reading a book or taking a class seems to place the Holy Spirit's power in the control of human hands.[2] (Again, see 1 Cor. 12:7–10.) NAR teaching on this point has more in common with New Age teachings than with biblical Christianity. Why do we say this? Because New Agers believe that everyone is born with supernatural powers they can "activate" or "awaken" or "unlock" by engaging in various New Age practices.[3]

Of course, it's also true that many practices promoted by NAR leaders—such the laying on of hands, fasting, and prayer—*are* found in the Bible.

There are instances when an apostle laid his hands on an individual and seemed to impart spiritual gifts (Acts 19:6; 1 Tim. 4:14; 2 Tim. 1:6). Notice, however, that in each of these instances, one of the original apostles played a key role in the impartation.[4] In the case of Timothy, where church elders were involved (1 Tim. 4:14), the apostle Paul was also present (2 Tim. 1:6). As we showed in chapter four, there is no scriptural evidence that there still exists an office of apostle. If it takes an apostle to impart a spiritual gift, those lined up today for the gifts they desire will be waiting a long time!

Teaching about practices like fasting and prayer are not new truths revealed through present-day apostles and prophets. These practices have characterized the church throughout its history. What is new are specific types of fasts and prayer supposedly revealed to NAR leaders.

---

[2]   Vinson Synan, "2000 Years of Prophecy," in *Understanding the Fivefold Ministry*, ed. Matthew D. Green (Lake Mary, FL: Charisma House, 2005), 55.

[3]   See, for example, these New Age sources: Rebecca Rosen, *Spirited: Unlock Your Psychic Self and Change Your Life* (NY: HarperCollins, 2010); and Doreen Virtue, *The Lightworker's Way: Awakening Your Spiritual Power to Know and Heal* (Carlsbad, CA: Hay House, 1997). For a Christian source on New Age teachings, see Douglas R. Groothuis, *Unmasking the New Age* (Downers Grove, IL: InterVarsity Press, 1986), 25–26.

[4]   Recall our definition of the apostles of Christ—they are those apostles mentioned in 1 Cor. 15:1–7 who had seen the resurrected Christ and operated with special authority in the first Christian era.

The Global Bridegroom Fast and 24/7 prayer rooms promoted by Mike Bickle's IHOP—these are novelties.

IHOP leaders suggest that participation in the Global Bridegroom Fast is needed for the fulfillment of God's end-time purposes, including the release of unprecedented miraculous power in the church. A statement on the IHOP website declares that the Global Bridegroom Fast was instituted directly by Jesus as a practice to continue until his Second Coming. "In January 2002, the word of the Lord came, saying, 'I am raising up a global bridegroom fast; ask Me to release one hundred million believers worldwide to come before Me in one accord for three days each month until I return.'"[5]

The purpose of the fast includes prayer for "spiritual breakthrough in the worldwide Church, with unprecedented unity, purity, and power"; "the great [end-time] harvest [of souls]"; and "fulfillment of all the prophetic promises to national Israel."[6] Thus, the Global Bridegroom Fast is a strategic, new practice essential to the church's mission in the world.[7]

The boast that a Global Bridegroom Fast is required of millions in the church is staggering. This is quite a revelation, one that places present-day apostles and prophets on a par with biblical apostles and prophets.

---

[5] "Global Bridegroom Fast," International House of Prayer; accessed December 3, 2013, http://www.ihopkc.org/about/global-bridegroom-fast. The statement does not say specifically to whom the word of the Lord came.

[6] Ibid.

[7] Fasting guidelines on the IHOP website state that fasting is always voluntary and can never be forced or made compulsory. But even though the Global Bridegroom Fast is not forced on particular individuals, it is still presented as a practice that must be embraced by many people in the church for God's end-time purposes to be realized. Thus, it is not a compulsory practice for a particular individual, but it does seem to be compulsory for the corporate church, or at least a large segment of it. See "Fasting Guidelines and Information," International House of Prayer; accessed February 23, 2014, http://www.ihopkc.org/about/fasting-guidelines-and-information.

Ditto for the practice of operating 24/7 prayer rooms. To say the least, prayer is a good thing. We applaud non-stop, round-the-clock praying by those who are so inclined. But Bickle teaches that this practice is not optional, saying, "Jesus *requires* night-and-day prayer for the full release of justice in the Church and society" [our emphasis].[8] He finds support for this in Luke 18:7–8: "And will not God give justice to his elect, who cry to him day and night? Will he delay long over them? I tell you, he will give justice to them speedily. Nevertheless, when the Son of Man comes, will he find faith on earth?"[9] But Bickle's interpretation neglects the context. And it ignores the fact that there is a much more reasonable way to read this passage. This isn't an appeal to erect non-stop, round-the-clock prayer rooms. It simply teaches that God will give justice to those who persist in prayer.

If we apply Bickle's methods of interpretation consistently, we get bizarre results. Joshua 1:8 and Psalm 1:2, for example, would be grounds for establishing 24/7 Bible reading rooms. (We hope no one thinks we're promoting a new, essential practice for the church! But it might not be a bad idea for people to read the Bible.) While Scripture reading is an essential practice for Christian maturity, establishing special rooms where Scripture is read non-stop, round-the-clock is not essential. The same holds for establishing special 24/7 prayer rooms.

---

8   Mike Bickle, "What the Spirit Is Saying About the Church," Mike Bickle.org; accessed May 6, 2014, http://www.mikebickle.org.edgesuite. net/MikeBickleVOD/2010/20101014_What_the_Holy_Spirit_Is_Emphasizing_in_this_Generation_IPP3.pdf, PDF file.

9   Ibid.

CAN PEOPLE GROW IN MIRACULOUS POWER UNTIL THEY OVERCOME SICKNESS AND DEATH AND EXECUTE GOD'S JUDGMENTS?

Some influential NAR leaders teach that their followers will grow in miraculous gifting until they can overcome sickness and death and execute God's judgments as described in the book of Revelation. Here again we encounter teachings that cannot be found in Scripture.

The teaching about overcoming sickness and death is based on a faulty interpretation of Romans 8:19–23. This passage does speak of an end-time event when Christians will experience the redemption of their mortal bodies into immortal bodies. But this redemption will not occur piecemeal or progressively as Christians accept new truths revealed by present-day apostles and prophets. Rather, this redemption will occur all at once and instantaneously (1 Cor. 15:52). And it will be accomplished solely by Christ, without the meddling of apostles or prophets, and quite apart from accepting any new truths taught by newly minted apostles and prophets. How wonderful the truth exclaimed by the apostle Paul: "But our citizenship is in heaven, and from it we await a Savior, the Lord Jesus Christ, who will transform our lowly body to be like his glorious body, by the power that enables him even to subject all things to himself" (Phil. 3:20–21).

Another NAR teaching (by Hamon) is that the church is a type of corporate Christ. The New Testament does use the phrase "Christ's body" as a metaphor for the church. This image depicts the reality that Christ indwells believers and works through the church. But it absolutely does not authorize the abhorrent idea that the church literally becomes Christ. Scripture also teaches that Christians become "partakers of the divine nature" (2 Peter 1:4). But this promises that Christians, indwelt by God's Holy Spirit, will be made into the image or likeness of Christ, so that they will become holy as well. The idea that human persons, born-again believers or not, can somehow attain deity—either individually or corporately—is a manifest heresy. We hope Hamon can demonstrate that this is not his view. We urge other NAR leaders, including those who warmly endorse Hamon's books, to demonstrate their solidarity with classical Christianity on these points. If they do not, then NAR followers may become confused about what they mean and fall into serious error.

Mike Bickle is to be praised for rejecting extreme expressions of the Manifest Sons of God doctrine. A statement on the IHOP website is helpful:

> We affirm that all born-again believers will be "manifest" as sons of God after the second coming of Christ.

> We deny that we will experience the fullness of our inheritance as sons of God before Jesus returns.

> Explanation: Some uphold the false teaching that in this age believers can have faith that will enable them to attain to qualities of life that are reserved only for believers in the resurrection.[10]

This point of clarification doesn't state which qualities of life are reserved for believers after Christ's return. Perhaps immortality is to be included. Bickle does claim to be forming an end-time movement of people who will develop unprecedented miraculous power and loose God's judgments on earth prior to Christ's return. These capacities are for the here-and-now and are not postponed until the resurrection of the saints. So there remains some mystery about his perspective on Manifest Sons of God teaching.

That end-time Christians will loose God's judgments cannot be supported by Scripture. Those scholars who believe that the church will join Christ in executing judgments on the nations (Rev. 19:14) also believe that the judgments have to do with spiritual warfare, not the passing of literal judgment. Others hold that, if these are literal judgments, then they will be loosed after Christ's return, not before. The question of timing matters, since the judgments will be

[10] Ernest Gruen and Mike Bickle, "Affirmations and Denials: Ernie Gruen and Mike Bickle's Joint Statement from 1993," International House of Prayer, May 16, 1993; accessed May 27, 2014, http://www.ihopkc.org/about/affirmations-and-denials.

executed under Christ's physically present leadership and direction after he returns.

Then, too, Christians will receive their glorified bodies and be completely free of sin. No sinful motivations will interfere with the execution of justice as the true sons of God join Christ in this sobering task.

Apparently, Bickle believes that Christians will loose judgments on unbelievers through their prayers prior to Christ's return and prior to their own glorification and complete sanctification. If true, it is a terrible truth, fraught with potential for abuse and the introduction of great injustice. Jesus rebuked James and John when they presumed to call down fire from heaven on people who had rejected Jesus (Luke 9:54–55).

★★★

In summary, there is no biblical support for NAR teachings about the rise of a miracle-working army that will perform greater miracles than those performed by Jesus or the apostles of Christ. Furthermore, Scripture nowhere suggests the notion of training miracle-workers. No place in Scripture encourages the belief that men and women may increase in miraculous power until they overcome sickness and death and execute God's judgments.

Conclusion

Our aim has been to follow the Berean example of Acts 17:10–12. When confronted with new teachings from the apostle Paul, the Bereans were open-minded and gave his teachings a fair hearing. But they didn't accept his teachings without question simply because he claimed to be an apostle. They checked them against the Scriptures to see if they lined up.

Likewise, we've done our best to give a fair hearing to the teachings being promoted today by leaders in the New Apostolic Reformation. We have also looked to Scripture to determine whether the teachings of these so-called modern apostles are true.

We've explained that NAR is a movement, not a formal organization. There is no official list of churches or leaders. Furthermore, not all people in the movement—not even all NAR leaders—hold to all the same beliefs.

The core NAR teaching, we believe, is that there are apostles and prophets today who exercise extraordinary authority in the lives of others and in the governance of the church. Their rationale for exercising such governing authority is that they're needed to unite Christians under their leadership and provide the church with new truths for the church to become a miracle-working army and thereby advance God's kingdom on earth. But we've shown that the Bible does not support these claims. It does not support their claim that NAR apostles and prophets have such authority over the church. Nor does it support their teaching that apostles and prophets have revealed new truths for the global church. In the Appendices following this conclusion, we offer suggestions for practical action, including "Advice for Parents, Pastors, and Participants in the New Apostolic Reformation" and "Questions to Ask of Churches."

But does it really matter whether people believe these things? Is any real harm done?

Certainly, some false beliefs are not as harmful as others. For example, it may not ultimately matter much if someone insists that church music must be a certain style. But false beliefs can be harmful when they have to do with more serious matters, such as the amount and type of authority that church leaders claim to have or how people should lead their lives and make important decisions.

We believe NAR teachings pose at least four dangers.

DEPENDENCY

One danger is that people will become overly dependent on apostles and prophets who exert unhealthy and unbiblical control over their lives. They may feel like they have to attend a church that is governed by an apostle lest they be outside God's will. Or they may believe that they should not make any major life decisions without first consulting a prophet. They might think they must obey the words of a prophet even if those words conflict with their own study of Scripture, the counsel of others who do not claim to be prophets or apostles, and simple common sense.

DISTRACTION AND DIMINISHED SPIRITUAL GROWTH

Another danger is that people will embrace NAR teachings and practices that are not supported by Scripture. At the very least, these teachings and practices are a distraction from true biblical teachings and practices and will stunt the spiritual maturity of those who embrace them. This stunting effect of NAR teachings is a sad irony since a major task of church leaders is to help Christians develop spiritual maturity. This is expressly stated in Ephesians 4:11–13, a passage cited especially frequently by NAR leaders.

> *And he gave the apostles, the prophets, the evangelists, the shepherds and teachers, to equip the saints for the work of ministry, for building up the body of Christ, until we all attain to the unity of the faith and of the knowledge of the Son of God, to mature manhood, to the measure of the stature of the fullness of Christ. . . .*

We shared a story about a man named Mike who felt like he must develop miraculous powers since otherwise he would be a failure as a Christian. Another part of his story we did not mention is that he held tightly to predictions he was given by prophets—predictions that, one day, he would stand on platforms and do "great exploits" of miracles—winning millions of people to God. Looking back, he believes that the prophecies fueled his ego and that he had become prideful. He also sees that he shaped a part his life around the prophecies, staying in the place he lived rather than moving to a different city to be closer to his young son because he thought moving would hinder the fulfillment of the prophecies. Mike now feels like he wasted crucial time going down a wrong track of NAR teachings, saying they "robbed me of a lot of years of maturity."

We know of remarkably similar cases where individuals, singled out for their talent, gifting, and visibility in the church and the world, have been advised through prophetic words that their ministries would extend beyond their present boundaries and reach tens of thousands and more. Some still expect this to happen. Others believe it has indeed happened through their speaking and writing. Some go to considerable effort seeking to make sure it happens.

DISILLUSIONMENT

When promises made by NAR leaders don't pan out—such as prophecies that a loved one will be healed or be preserved from death—many people grow disillusioned. Some conclude that God has failed them and they experience years of anger or resentment toward God. These are people who believe that God made a promise and failed to deliver. At best, they struggle to find meaning in prayer. Their fellowship with other believers seems hollow. For some, their disillusionment escalates into general distrust of the church and real doubts about the truth of Christianity.

Others in the New Apostolic Reformation tire of trying to stay afloat on the endless stream of new truths that are being revealed by the apostles and prophets. One former participant in NAR recalls the spiritual fatigue he experienced. Kyle says he felt like he was following a "moving target." But at the same time, Kyle believed he couldn't afford to miss the latest truth lest he miss out on experiencing God's blessings in his life.

DIVISION

NAR beliefs also divide, as church-goers and family members are forced to make painful choices between maintaining peace and adhering to Scripture as their solid base of common ground and authoritative source of knowledge. Brothers and sisters in Christ—who are also, sometimes, literal brothers and sisters—experience tension because those who follow NAR apostles and prophets have been taught to see those who don't as less spiritual, or, even worse, as spiritual enemies.

We've tried to show that the teachings of the New Apostolic Reformation depart from the beliefs of long-standing Christian traditions, including those of Pentecostals and charismatics. If our analysis of this movement is correct, then Christians must be wary of association with it and be alert to its infiltration of our churches.

We urge readers to study the Scriptures carefully and to test NAR claims as the Bereans did. The Bereans' investigative zeal is a model for the church today. If supposed apostles and prophets are correct in their teachings, they have nothing to lose when their claims are tested against the sure word of God in Scripture. But if they are incorrect, their followers have much to lose.

Some NAR leaders will be vexed by a thorough examination of their claims. But we confidently assure you that God will not be displeased if you question the genuineness of a so-called apostle or prophet. Rather, God will honor your desire and determination to be as discerning as possible. And he has made provision for discernment in his revealed Word, the Spirit-inspired Scriptures.

Appendix A

Advice for Parents, Pastors, and Participants in the New Apostolic Reformation

Once people have learned about the New Apostolic Reformation, they often wonder how they should respond. They wonder what they might say to loved ones involved with this movement. They wonder whether they should warn others about the movement, and how to go about it if they believe they should. Some may realize that they have, unwittingly, adopted NAR beliefs and wonder what to do about it now. In all these situations, seeking God's direction through prayer is indispensable. Beyond that, here are a few more suggestions.

ADVICE TO PARENTS
(OR SPOUSES, OR SIBLINGS, OR OTHER LOVED ONES)

A parent may be alarmed that a child has moved in the direction of embracing NAR beliefs. If this is your concern, then it's important, first, to clarify what your child actually believes. It's best not to jump to conclusions.

It's easy for people, including Christians, to talk past one another because they assume they know what the other person thinks. We have to work at truly understanding. For example, what does your child mean when referring to so-and-so as an apostle? It could be that your child's view of some church leader's authority is quite different than that leader's view of his or her own authority. Knowing that may help you approach your child one way rather than another. The best way to understand your child's new perspective is to ask questions. And the best way to demonstrate your desire to understand is to ask with gentleness and respect.

You may not need to convince your child that no one today has the same level of authority as the apostles of Christ. Your child may already agree with you on that point. Instead you may need to show that a particular leader does consider himself an apostle, equal in authority with the apostles of Christ. You will want to gather samples of that apostle's teaching materials and discuss them with your child to help give him or her a clearer view of what that leader claims and teaches.

It's critical that you listen closely to your child's concerns and convictions. Be sensitive to any challenges and the specific reasons for that child's attraction to NAR teachings. Do your own homework to make sure you're knowledgeable about NAR doctrines and practices that appeal to the child. And always be careful to respond calmly and patiently.

You may hear your child speak language typical of NAR communities. If you hear language and terminology we've described in this book, encourage the child to clarify. This will enlarge your understanding of your child's perspective. And it may get the child thinking about what he or she believes in a more careful fashion than before. Sometimes just getting people to think more carefully about certain teachings will result in greater discernment about other new teachings they encounter.

So first, clarify what your child believes—for both your sakes.

Second, ask your child to support any questionable new beliefs from Scripture. If you hear a verse used incorrectly, show why you think that understanding of the verse misses the target. You should point out that quoting a verse without reference to its context and the rest of what Scripture teaches isn't good practice. It may take some effort to be understood correctly, but that is our responsibility when contemplating the things of God.

Even if they don't seem to be listening, continue to challenge your children with Scripture. Don't be content with quoting Scripture;

find ways to communicate the meaning of any passage you quote. Sometimes a paraphrase that accurately captures the point is helpful.

Stock your personal library with reliable commentaries. Let your children see the care you take in studying the Scriptures for the truth it yields. If your family attends church together, invite your children to reflect on the messages they hear. Ask them what they think. Do they agree with sermon? Is there something they didn't understand? Were they puzzled by anything that was said? Did the preacher make sense? Follow up with more questions. Probe for specifics. Hold off sharing your own opinion until later—unless your child asks. This is a time to get better acquainted with your child, to encourage reflection, to assist in developing critical skills and a respect for Scripture. This is effective only if your child knows you respect his intellect and doesn't feel as if you're cross-examining him for orthodoxy. Build trust in the way you demonstrate your interest.

Our experience has been that parents who fear that their children have wandered into dangerous paths often discover that what they've been taught stays with them and always beckons them to return. By God's grace and the help of the Holy Spirit, you've planted seeds that will sprout later. Remember that God's Word is not like mere human words, but rather is living and dynamic. It has the power to expose any error or evil we have embraced, as it is "sharper than any two-edged sword, piercing to the division of soul and of spirit, of joints and of marrow, and discerning the thoughts and intentions of the heart" (Heb. 4:12).

So clarify and gently challenge. Appeal to Scripture without being preachy. Invite a sharing of ideas. Do all of this with grace. Communicate the value of thinking independently and responsibly. Let your child know that you love and accept him no matter what. This is critical. People in NAR are often taught that those who oppose NAR teachings are motivated by an evil spirit or are jealous of NAR leaders. Many apostles and prophets show disdain for those who question, challenge, or disagree with them. This will set off an alarm for any child whose parents have consistently spoken grace and peace into their lives. If they detect a judgmental spirit from you, they will not see clearly how this differs from anything they experience among NAR folk.

You must be more gracious than your critics. It will be more difficult to dismiss you as evil—and write off your concerns about NAR teachings—if you act with kindness and gentleness, even toward those with whom you disagree (see 1 Pet. 3:15–16).

If your children know you love them, they may realize that any apostles and prophets who have demonized you—and all others who question their teachings—have mischaracterized you. That realization alone may be the key that makes them wary of NAR dogmas: it may cause them to check for other false things taught by these leaders.

You can demonstrate to your child that true Christian belief shows itself in love—not in disdain for others who believe differently than we do. Love is a sign of the Holy Spirit's influence in a person's life (Gal. 5:23)—even more than the working of miracles—and is the most important character trait (1 Cor. 13). It is a crucial test of whether someone is truly a believer (1 John 4:20), more so for anyone who claims to be an apostle or prophet.

Seeing your good behavior—in contrast to any apostles or prophets who don't have regard for their fellow believers—may win your child over as much as your words (see 1 Peter 3:1). Paul counseled Timothy to "Keep a close watch on yourself and on the teaching. Persist in this, for by so doing you will save both yourself and your hearers," in this case your children (1 Tim. 4:16).

A word of encouragement to parents of young children. You have opportunities to teach your children discernment and to instill reasoning skills for the days ahead. Believers will always be challenged by competing worldviews. You can foster in your children a respect for God's Word and a commitment to test "every wind of doctrine" (Eph. 4:14) against the pages of Scripture. Plant seeds of wisdom now and look forward to a harvest in the days ahead.

Advice to Pastors

If you are a pastor or church leader, or a layperson who has been given a teaching platform, we encourage you to use your influence to warn people about the encroachment of NAR teachings in churches. You're in a position to inform them of its teachings and explain how they deviate from Scripture.

First, familiarize yourself with the movement and NAR interpretations of Scripture used to support key teachings. This book is a good place to start. Our other book, *A New Apostolic Reformation? A Biblical Response to a Worldwide Movement* (Weaver Book Company, 2014), provides greater detail and a fuller assessment of the movement.

Second, don't wait for your flock to come to you with questions. Be proactive. Teach your people to be on the lookout for NAR teachings. Many Christians haven't heard of the New Apostolic Reformation. The trend in churches is to avoid directly confronting from the pulpit specific belief systems or identifying individuals who actively promote harmful teachings. But this is a disservice to your flock. The apostle Paul admonished the elders of the church in Ephesus to guard their flock against false teachings (Acts 20:28–31). The need today is for courageous leaders like Paul, who are not shy about teaching God's Word—even when it is unpopular and may offend some people (Acts 20:26–27). But your ministry of teaching and warning needs also to communicate love and grace.

Understand that NAR leaders move into places where they think opportunity is greatest and resistance will be minimal. For this reason, those who attend Pentecostal or charismatic churches are perhaps more likely to encounter NAR teachings. There is an urgent need for instruction about how NAR doctrines and practices differ from traditional Pentecostal and charismatic teachings. For example, one Vineyard church may steer clear of this movement while another experiments, or even identifies, with it. There are Pentecostal and charismatic communities whose leaders are concerned that individual churches are aligning with NAR teachings and activities. This is one reason why we've written this book.

We also encourage leaders within a congregation to have conversations with each other about these matters. One may discover that another is drawn to NAR. The sooner this becomes known, the better it will be for the congregation. For that matter, we urge others in the church to go to their leaders and ask about their views about apostles and prophets, to ask carefully crafted and direct questions about NAR teachings in relation to their own church. (See Appendix B for more on this.)

Finally, we urge you to watch for signs in your congregation that some are attracted to NAR teachings and practices. We've learned that deliberate infiltration is not uncommon. Take care not to lend a platform to those with aberrant beliefs. Be especially vigilant on behalf of the young people in your church. And take care to vet potential leaders for any affiliation they may have with the NAR.

We believe that if more pastors confronted NAR teachings with sound doctrine anchored in the Word of God, this movement would not be gaining such a foothold in today's churches.

Advice to Participants in NAR

Some people are surprised to learn they've been attending a church that is part of the New Apostolic Reformation. They may unwittingly have adopted some NAR beliefs as their own. And then they hear a message or read a book like this one and recognize that much of what they've heard and been taught is a central feature of NAR. It occurs to them that these beliefs and practices simply do not hold up when examined in the light of Scripture.

You may want to separate yourself from a movement that is playing with fire, but you aren't sure how. You may be confused and even a little fearful, especially if you've spent many years under NAR teaching. Here are a few suggestions.

First, it's imperative that you commit to reading the Bible as the original writers intended for it to be understood. If you've sat under NAR teachings for any length of time, you may have picked up faulty methods for interpreting Scripture. For example, you may have been casual in accepting this or that apostle's claims about the "deeper meaning" of a passage, when you should be examining the passage for what it plainly says. Don't feel ashamed if you need to relearn how to read the Bible. Personal Bible study is the path to great discovery and knowledge of God. A good book to begin with is *How to Read the Bible for All Its Worth*, by Gordon D. Fee and Douglas Stuart (Zondervan).

Second, commit to learning sound theology so that you can spot bad theology when you see it. Despite what you may have been taught, theology is not a part of "dead religion" or a "Greek mindset." It's merely good thinking about God. Good thinking is thinking that results in believing what's true. So ask yourself, are you good at believing the things you do?

Learning more about God should be a lifelong process filled with joy. Your first step in developing sound theology is getting acquainted with *all* of God's Word. Read broadly and in context. Get a good study Bible so you can understand the historical and cultural background of what you read. Beyond that, another step is to read books of an introductory nature, like *Christian Beliefs: Twenty Basics Every Christian Should Know*, by Wayne Grudem (Zondervan). Or, to go even deeper, take advantage of a free online resource called "The Theology Program." This is a step-by-step, comprehensive program in theology at a seminary level, without the cost or relocation required to attend a traditional seminary. Visit the website at https://bible.org/article/theology-program.

Third, if you've encountered NAR teachings that demonize anyone who questions their apostles and prophets, then you might need to upgrade your reasoning skills and overcome some anxiety. Many people who once embraced NAR teachings fear they will be subject to God's anger for abandoning them. A good resource for you is *Twisted Scriptures: Breaking Free from Churches That Abuse,* by Mary Alice Chrnalogar (Zondervan).

Fourth, find a healthy church with a demonstrated emphasis on teaching though the Bible and nurturing believers with life application. If your experience has soured you on church, you may be tempted to withdraw from church completely, fearful of exposure to further deception. But it's imperative for you to be involved with a strong fellowship of believers who are jointly committed to growing a mature and discerning faith. You can supplement the teaching you receive from your local church with excellent teaching from nationally known teachers whose messages air on radio, are streamed on the Internet, or are available as podcasts.

Fifth, you can find encouragement from other Christians who have left NAR. If you can't find these people in your new church, many such people can be found online on Christian discussion boards and blogs. Reaching out to other people who have had similar experiences in NAR may help you find your footing. Holly Pivec operates a blog called *Spirit of Error,* which examines NAR. You may find this resource helpful (www.spiritoferror.org).

Appendix B

Questions to Ask of Churches

How can you know if a particular church or organization is associated with NAR?

Finding the answer may not be as easy as looking at the marquee in front of the church or reading its statement of faith. Many NAR groups have adopted fairly standard statements that do not mention their NAR teachings, and it can take some time attending a church before you recognize signs of NAR influence.

Asking people in the organization if it's part of the New Apostolic Reformation may not be very illuminating, either. Many people—even those involved with this movement—don't know it by its formal name. It won't do to walk into a church and ask, "Is this church part of the New Apostolic Reformation?" Even if it is, people there may wonder what you're talking about.

One clue is the use of terminology. The phrase *fivefold ministry* is prominent in the teaching of NAR leaders and sympathizers. (See our explanation of this term in chapter 2.) Though not all people who speak of the fivefold ministry hold to NAR beliefs, many do.[1] So this is a clue to probe more deeply. Use of the terms *apostle* and *prophet*—also, the adjectives *apostolic* and *prophetic*—to refer to church leaders is another clue. And of course, if the church or organization promotes books and other literature written by influential apostles and prophets—such as Rick Joyner, Bill Johnson, or Cindy Jacobs—that may be another indicator.

---

[1] We note that the term *fivefold ministry* sometimes is used outside of the New Apostolic Reformation, often by Pentecostal Christians, to refer to the belief that God has given some people the spiritual gifts (not church governing offices) of apostle, prophet, evangelist, pastor, and teacher.

If you're still unsure where a church or organization stands on NAR issues, here are some questions you can ask the leaders to help you gauge their views.

- Do you believe that some people alive today are apostles and prophets? (If the answer is yes, then you should seek clarification.) What do you mean by *apostles* and *prophets*? (See the next set of questions.)

- Do you believe that today's apostles and prophets share similar authority and functions to the apostles of Christ and the Old Testament prophets? Do they have the authority to govern churches and to reveal new truths (also known as present truth)? If not, what do you believe about them? Are apostles similar to missionaries and church planters, or do they also have a greater authority to govern the church? Are prophets simply people who have the spiritual gift of prophecy or something more?

- Does the leader of this church consider himself or herself to be an apostle or prophet?

- If this church is governed by a pastor, then is it part of a larger apostolic network of churches that has come under the authority of an apostle?

- Do you believe that, for God's kingdom to advance, Christians must cast out territorial spirits (high-ranking demons that rule over cities and nations)?

- Does this church promote practices of strategic-level spiritual warfare, including spiritual mapping, prayerwalking, and the Seven Mountain Mandate? (If the answer is yes to any of these questions, you'll want clarification. You should ask: What exactly do you mean by these practices? Recall from chapter 8 that some churches engage in prayerwalking, but they do not view their practice as an attempt to cast out territorial spirits.)

- Does this church teach that people can learn to work miracles? More specifically, does it offer classes or promote books that teach people to work miracles?

When asking questions like these, there is something important to keep in mind. After reading this book you have a framework for understanding NAR that many people—even many church leaders—do not have. They may not have thought about the distinctions, say, between the governing office of prophet and the spiritual gift of prophecy, or the exact purpose of a prayerwalk conducted by their church. Be prepared to explain what you mean when you use these terms. It might be helpful to review the sections of this book that explain the NAR definitions of these terms and compare them with how they're used by more long-standing church traditions.

One more thing. When you get a hint that someone in your church or organization has adopted a NAR perspective, ask that person for more information. Ask specifically how he or she learned about these things. You must ask with genuine interest. Find out if there's a book the person has read, or a church the person has visited, or an event the person has attended, that would explain their enthusiasm for NAR-type views and activities. You will know from reading this book which names, organizations, and places to listen for. You might then want to ask how this person's views have been received in the church, especially by its leaders.

Appendix C

Name-Calling

One unfortunate practice that is seen frequently in the New Apostolic Reformation is the use of disparaging labels. Many NAR leaders respond to those who question or challenge their teachings by calling them insulting names. You may hear them accuse a person of having an evil heart that is opposed to the things and people of God. The implication is that God is displeased with that person.

One harmful effect of this practice of demonizing people who question NAR leaders is that it dulls the critical thinking abilities of people in NAR. People who were once affiliated with the movement often report that they always felt pressure to go along, to accept pretty much anything an apostle or prophet said, if only to avoid being labeled with an insulting name.

No one should worry that God will think he has an evil heart or be displeased if he questions the teachings of someone who claims to be an apostle or a prophet. Our perfectly loving Savior and Lord will not discipline us or be displeased with us if we're cautious about accepting someone's claim to be a genuine apostle or prophet—especially when the Word of God specifically warns us to be cautious and not to be taken in by false apostles and prophets.

Following is a list of nine insulting names often applied to those who challenge NAR apostles and prophets.

1. *Critical spirit,* as in "She has a critical spirit." (Translation: Since she is challenging a NAR leader, she is mean and enjoys criticizing people.)

2. *Greek mindset,* as in "He has a Greek mindset." (Translation: Anything "Greek" is associated with logic, philosophy, and

academia, and it is inferior, untrustworthy, or simply bad. In contrast, the "Hebrew mindset" is the spiritual and more mystical view, and is not bound by logic or academic study. Thus, the Hebrew mindset is truer to God's heart.)

3. *Jezebel spirit,* as in "She has a Jezebel spirit." (Translation: She is persecuting the prophets just like evil Queen Jezebel did.)

4. *Legalist,* as in "He is a legalist." (Translation: He only cares about what is written in the Bible and isn't open to the new things God is doing today through the apostles and prophets.)

5. *Old wineskin,* as in "That church is part of the old wineskin." (Translation: They are stuck in what God did in the past and haven't caught up with what he is doing today through the apostles and prophets.)

6. *Pharisee,* as in "He is a Pharisee." (Translation: He only cares about doctrine and is not open to a new work of God through NAR.)

7. *Religious spirit,* as in "The people in that church have a religious spirit." (Translation: That church is only interested in the old revelation contained in the Bible and is not open to new truths from NAR apostles and prophets.)

8. *Spirit of Saul,* as in "That person has a spirit of Saul." (Translation: That person is not chosen by God to lead and is persecuting the apostles and prophets God has chosen to lead.)

9. *Unanointed,* as in "That pastor is totally unanointed." (Translation: That pastor has not been chosen by God to lead, just like King Saul was not chosen to lead Israel, but instead David was—and as NAR apostles and prophets are chosen to lead the church!)

Glossary

This glossary focuses on key terms related to the New Apostolic Reformation (NAR) that are used in this book.

activation. A NAR teaching that miraculous gifts of the Holy Spirit, such as healing and prophesying, can be activated (or released) in individuals who embrace new truths that have been revealed by NAR apostles and prophets.

apostolic network. An entity in which the pastors of multiple churches have submitted to the authority of a single apostle or group of apostles.

apostolic unity. A NAR teaching that Christian unity is achieved through Christians' submission to the leadership of apostles.

dominionism. A NAR teaching that the church must yield to the authority of modern-day apostles and prophets to whom God has given new strategies to advance his kingdom.

ecclesiastical apostles. NAR apostles who govern churches and ministries.

fivefold ministry. A NAR teaching that God has given the church five continuing governmental offices (apostle, prophet, evangelist, pastor, and teacher).

generational curse. A curse that has been passed on from a parent to a child. These curses often result when one's ancestor engaged in some type of false religious practice or sinful activity.

Great End-Time Harvest. A popular NAR prophecy that, in the end time, more than a billion people will convert to belief in Christ—including entire nations—making this event the greatest harvest of souls in history. It will occur as a result of the implementation of new spiritual warfare practices being revealed by NAR apostles and prophets. It will also occur as a result of miraculous signs that will be performed by NAR apostles, prophets, and their followers.

Great End-Time Transfer of Wealth. A popular NAR prophecy that, in the end time, the wealth of the wicked people of the world will supernaturally flow to the church so it can be used to advance God's kingdom.

healing rooms. Specially appointed places located in churches or communities where people who are ill can go to receive prayer for their physical healing. The people who run these rooms often engage in NAR practices for the activation of the miraculous gifts.

Joel's Army. A NAR teaching that the rise of a church-army, led by end-time apostles and prophets, is prophetically foretold in Joel 2.

laying on of hands. A NAR practice whereby an apostle or prophet lays hands on an individual for the purpose of transferring to that individual a miraculous gift possessed by that apostle or prophet, such as a gift of healing or prophesying.

Manifest Sons of God. A NAR teaching that those who follow the end-time apostles and prophets will become manifest (or revealed) as sons of God, patterned after the original Son of God, Jesus Christ. They will work the same miracles—and even greater miracles—than Jesus did. Those who embrace extreme expressions of this teaching believe they'll continue to grow in miraculous power until they execute God's judgments on earth and overcome sickness and death.

many-membered man-child. A NAR teaching that the church, under the leadership of end-time apostles and prophets, will become a type of corporate Christ—a literal extension of the incarnation of Christ on earth.

New Apostolic Reformation. A movement within Protestant Christianity—and particularly rising out of independent charismatic churches—that seeks to restore the "lost" church offices of apostle and prophet. People in this movement believe that modern-day apostles and prophets must hold official offices in church government.

new truths. New teachings and practices that have been revealed by NAR apostles and prophets.

prayerwalking. A NAR practice of sending teams of individuals to the physical locations of regions where they desire to see spiritual and societal transformation. At these locations, the teams engage in warfare prayer and other practices of strategic-level spiritual warfare.

prophetic acts. Various NAR practices that are intended to release God's power, such as driving into the ground stakes inscribed with passages of Scripture or anointing a property with oil.

prophetic illumination. A NAR teaching that God gives modern-day prophets supernatural insight into the correct interpretation and application of a specific passage of Scripture. The prophet's new understanding of the passage was not known by the church before it was revealed to the prophet.

receiving a prophet. A NAR practice of accepting the words of a NAR prophet as the very words of God.

Seven Mountain Mandate. A new strategy for advancing God's kingdom that God has revealed to NAR apostles and prophets. According to this revelation, the church must take control of the seven most influential societal institutions—called *mountains*—which are identified as government, media, family, business, education, church, and arts.

soaking. A NAR practice intended to help individuals experience greater intimacy with God. Soaking often involves elements such as finding a place of solitude, praying in one's native language, and speaking in tongues, and then waiting to experience God's presence in a tangible way, such as by having a vision, an out-of-body experience, or angelic visitation.

spiritual covering. A NAR practice whereby pastors and all other individuals are expected to submit to an apostle in return for receiving spiritual protection and blessing from God. This practice is also referred to as seeking apostolic covering.

spiritual mapping. A NAR practice of creating a spiritual profile of a city or nation to help identify which powerful demon is ruling over that particular geographical region.

strategic-level spiritual warfare. The NAR act of confronting powerful evil spirits that are believed to rule specific regions of the world.

supernatural school of ministry. NAR schools, often administered by churches, where students are trained to work miracles, such as healing people and prophesying. These schools are also sometimes referred to as schools of the Holy Spirit or schools of prophets.

Treasure Hunt. A NAR practice in which a team of three or four people goes into a community and asks God to give them *clues* about people they'll find in the community. They mark these clues on a *treasure map*, which they use to guide them to a person—called a *treasure*—who matches their clues. Treasure Hunts are a form of supernatural evangelism—also called prophetic evangelism—in which participants rely on miraculous gifts of the Holy Spirit, including prophecy and healing, to share God's love with people.

24/7 prayer rooms. Specially appointed places located in churches or communities where participants engage in the practice of non-stop, round-the-clock prayer. Typically, the participants sign up to pray in shifts, covering certain blocks of time.

warfare prayer. The NAR practice of issuing direct commands to powerful evil spirits that rule cities and nations, including commanding them to leave those regions.

workplace apostles. NAR apostles who govern what they call the church in the workplace—that is, they govern the Christians who work in various sectors of society, like business, media, and government.

Name Index

Subject Index

abortion, *96*

activating miraculous gifts, *48, 104, 114, 118, 143*

Agabus, *56, 57*

Aglow International (Edmonds, Washington), *6*

Ahijah the Shilonite, *53*

Almolonga, Guatemala, *96–97*

Amos, *54*

Ananias, *34*

Andronicus, *24*

angel feathers, *xv*

animal noises, *xv*

Anna, *56*

"another Jesus", *27*

Apollyon (territorial spirit), *88*

apostles
   authority of, *8, 10–12*
   characteristics of, *15–16*
   commissioned by Christ, *22, 33, 35–36*
   flexible range of meaning, *25, 32–33*
   governing churches, *4, 8–14, 29–31*
   life and ministry of, *40–41*
   NAR use of term, *137*
   as temporary office, *8, 31–32, 41*
   testing of, *33–41*

"apostles of Christ", *25–26, 28, 32, 36, 119n4, 138*

"apostles of the churches", *26, 28*

Apostolic Age, *20, 26, 33*

Apostolic Council of Prophetic Elders, *45–46*

apostolic covering, *11*

apostolic networks, *10–11, 97–98, 143*

apostolic teachings, *74*

apostolic unity, *96–101, 143*

Arminianism, *98*

Asherah, prophets of, *59*

Assemblies of God, *9nn1–2*

Athanasius, *33*

Australian Coalition of Apostles and Prophets, *17*

Baal, prophets of, *59*

Barnabas, *24, 57*

Bereans, *xiii, 38–39, 125, 128*

Bethel Church (Redding, California), *xv, 6, 104, 106*

bodies, glorification of, *108, 124*

Brazilian Coalition of Apostles, *17*

Call, The, *6, 96*

Calvinism, *98*

Canadian Coalition of Apostles, *17*

cessationists, *43*

Charisma magazine, *6, 45, 48*

charismatics, mainstream, *xiv, 9n1, 43, 104, 128*

children, trained to work miracles, *105–6*

Christian International Ministries Network, *6*

Christian unity, *98, 99–101*

Scripture Index

Amos
1:1 *62*
3:7 *47*

Micah
3:5 *75*

3:5–12 *59*
3:11 *75*

New Testament

Matthew
7:15 *59, 76*
7:16–23 *75*
10:1–7 *35*
10:2 *18*
10:2–4 *18*
10:41 *70*
24:11 *59*
24:24 *60, 74*
28:16–20 *18*

Luke
1:2 *20*
1:41–45 *58*
1:46–55 *58*
1:67–79 *58*
2:28–32 *58*
9:54–55 *124*
10:17–19 *92*
18:7–8 *121*
24:13–34 *117*
24:25–27 *53*
24:44 *117*
24:45 *117*

John
14:12 *110, 115–16*
14:26 *20*
15:26–27 *20*
17:20–23 *99*
17:21 *99*
17:23 *99*

Acts
1:3–8 *21*
1:8 *35*
1:15–26 *19*
1:21–22 *19*
1:24–26 *35*
2:11 *58*
2:14–47 *19*
2:42 *20*
2:43 *19*
2:44–47 *99*
3:4–8 *19*
4:32–37 *19*
4:34–37 *7*
5:1–11 *19*
5:12 *19*
5:15 *37*
6:1–6 *19*
8:39–40 *114*
10:39–41 *19*
11:28–30 *57*
13:1–3 *57*
13:1–22 *25*
13:2–3 *24*
13:6–8 *60*
13:10 *75*
14:3 *23*
14:4 *24*
14:14 *24*
15:2 *20*
15:6 *20*
15:22 *57*
15:22–23 *20*

15:32 *57*
15:40 *24*
16:19–21 *116*
17:6 *116*
17:10–12 *xiii, 38, 125*
17:11 *38*
19:6 *119*
19:11–12 *23*
19:23–29 *116*
20:26–27 *133*
20:28–31 *133*
26:16–18 *21*

Romans
1:4 *40*
1:5 *22*
1:16 *23, 117*
2:5 *65*
8:19–23 *111, 122*
11:13 *22*
15:19 *23*
16:7 *24*
16:17 *24n3*

1 Corinthians
1:2–16 *100*
1:11–12 *99*
1:18 *117*
1:22–24 *117*
1:26–31 *117*
3:4 *101*
5:4–5 *23*
9:1 *22, 31, 34*